To Nadau —

Enjoy!

MARK

Advance Praise for *The 40 Day Challenge*

Pithy and powerful, Rabbi Wildes takes us on a 40 day journey to becoming a better version of ourselves.

> – Charlie Harary, Motivational Speaker
> and Author of *Unlocking Greatness*

I love this book and how Rabbi Wildes has created an engaging, easy-to-read, and downright inspiring daily challenge. The anecdotes he cites are relevant, timely, and touching.... I wholeheartedly recommend it.

> – Moshe Kinderlehrer, Publisher of the
> *Jewish Link of NJ / Expanded Edition*

What a brilliant resource for scholars and laymen alike to make the forty days between Elul and Yom Kippur not only meaningful, but poignant and transformative.

> – Dr. Nava R. Silton, Fox 5 Psychological Correspondent

Rabbi Wildes offers an inspiring and practical field guide that will help readers take full advantage of a period on the Jewish calendar earmarked for unparalleled growth and Divine mercy.

> – Yehoshua November, Author of L.A. Times
> Book Finalist *God's Optimism*

Rabbi Wildes guides us to become the best version of ourselves. The 40 Day Challenge is recommended reading – not just during Elul and the Days of Awe, but for the rest of the year as well.

> – Julian Horowitz, founding member and
> Music Director of The Maccabeats

THE 40 DAY CHALLENGE

DAILY INSIGHTS TO PREPARE FOR THE HIGH HOLIDAYS

RABBI MARK WILDES

KODESH PRESS

THE 40 DAY CHALLENGE:
Daily Insights to Prepare for the High Holidays

© Manhattan Jewish Experience (MJE), 2021

Hardcover ISBN: 978-1-947857-68-1
Paperback ISBN: 978-1-947857-67-4

Kodesh Press LLC
New York, NY
www.kodeshpress.com
kodeshpress@gmail.com
sales@kodeshpress.com

Set in Arno Pro by Raphaël Freeman MISTD, Renana Typesetting
Printed in the United States of America

Thank you to the following MJE sponsors for their generosity and support enabling the publication of *The 40 Day Challenge:*

> *Ann Arbesfeld in memory Hyman Arbesfeld z"l*
> *Leon and Alice Wildes*
> *David and Sarah Green*
> *Robyn and Shukie Grossman*
> *Michael and Amy Wildes*
> *Eddie Zarabi*
> *Andrew and Shannon Penson*
> *Tammy Wolchok*
> *Yossi Mervis*
> *Casey Levine*
> *Yudi and Shira Teichman*
> *Jonathan and Amy Baron*
> *David and Alex Segal*
> *Liezel Huber*
> *Serge and Kaylee Zenin*
> *Barry and Joy Sklar*

In the merit of their kindness and love for Torah, Jewish education and outreach, may they and their families be blessed with a sweet new year of good health, prosperity and spiritual growth.

Contents

Introduction

IN AMERICAN POP CULTURE, SUPERBOWL SUNDAY RISES TO the level of holiday status. Besides the tens of thousands who prepare for the day by spending top dollar on travel and tickets, millions of Americans take the time to plan where and with whom they will watch "the big game." You can only imagine the intense preparation taken by the actual players themselves.

One player stands out when it comes to preparing for the Super Bowl – Tom Brady, the famed quarterback who competed in ten Super Bowls, seven of which he won. In February of 2021, at the age of forty-three, Brady led his new team – the Tampa Bay Buccaneers – to victory and was elected MVP. All that is well known. What is less known is the extent to which Tom Brady prepared.

Although by this time Brady had already won six Super Bowls, to prepare for the 2021 game Brady sent scouting tips and films to his players at all hours of the night. He followed a strict diet, sleep, and workout routine from which he never veered. One teammate told reporters that Brady convinced him to meet for workouts at 5:30 a.m., and when he once showed at 6:30 a.m., Brady greeted him sarcastically with the words: "Good afternoon." Also, even though the Super Bowl was held in Brady's home stadium in Tampa and he was therefore able to stay home, his training was so intense that his family moved out for the two weeks before the game so he could prepare without any interruption.

Any successful person will agree – nothing can replace proper preparation. Thomas Edison, the well-known inventor, famously said: "Genius is 1 percent inspiration and 99 percent perspiration." Nothing takes the place of hard work, training, and preparation.

Why should the same discipline not be exerted in our spiritual pursuits?

Each year, Jews of all backgrounds attend High Holiday services – the Super Bowl of all prayer services. For some, Rosh Hashanah and Yom Kippur are powerful spiritual experiences, but for many others, it feels like something is missing. Maybe we blame the rabbi for being less than inspirational or we don't like the tunes the cantor chose to sing. But what could we do *ourselves* to get more out of the High Holiday experience?

Like every other part of life, we must prepare! To get a high from the High Holidays, to truly experience the holiness of these "days of awe," we must train in some way. What meaningful experience have you ever enjoyed that "just happened" without some advance preparation? "There can be no holiness without preparation." This quote by Rabbi Joseph B. Soloveitchik, one of the great Jewish thinkers of the twentieth century, lies at the heart of Judaism and sums up why I decided to write this book.

When the Jewish people gathered at Mount Sinai to receive the Torah, they weren't told to just "show up." God instructed them to take a few days to prepare for this special divine encounter. And to this day, Jews, every year, count forty-nine days from the festival of Passover to Shavuot, as a way to prepare for the day the Jewish people celebrate this event in our history. Rabbi Chaim ibn Attar (1696–1743), in his monumental biblical commentary, *Or Ha-Chaim*, asked: If God took the Jews out of Egypt in order to give them the Torah, then why did He not do so immediately? Why did God wait seven weeks before gathering His people at Sinai and only then reveal to them the Torah? The *Or Ha-Chaim* answered that the Jews needed time to prepare, to shake off the dust of Egyptian slavery. They needed a period of adjustment and maturation to transition from being slaves to receiving the Torah. So, God waited and gave our ancestors some time to prepare.

Our lives today are no different. There are special events that transform the trajectory of our lives. It could be an interview for that job we've always wanted or a romantic evening when we finally propose to that special someone. These occasions alter our life path in profound ways, which is why we don't just show up and see what happens. We dedicate time to prepare. We rehearse what we're going to say at the next client meeting, how we will show our loved one we truly care about them, or what we want to say to a friend who is going through a difficult time. We don't just appear on scene without a plan. Yet year after year, we show up on Rosh Hashanah and Yom Kippur and expect to be swept away by the magic of the moment. We have, however, been given a time period to prepare for the High Holidays – a forty-day period beginning on Rosh Chodesh Elul – the first day of the holiest month of the Jewish year. If we take advantage of this time period, I believe our High Holidays and our overall Jewish experience all year would be profoundly transformed for the better.

During the pandemic, as everyone began to distance themselves from one another, I was looking for a way to stay connected. I wanted to remain in touch with my students and friends and keep them spiritually energized, especially as the High Holidays were approaching. And so, besides the daily Zoom and Facebook Live classes offered by the Manhattan Jewish Experience (MJE),* I started a WhatsApp challenge group. The "challenge" consisted of Torah insights to be listened to each day, from Rosh Chodesh Elul to Yom Kippur. Hundreds of people joined and became regular listeners, and when the forty days were up, I was already in a groove, and so I just kept going every day, in fact, to this day. It's been a great journey and a wonderful way for me to start my day each morning. One of my students suggested I write up these forty entries and hence the idea for this publication, *The Forty-Day Challenge*, was born.

Take a few moments each day to read one entry. Then answer the challenge question that follows so you can apply what you've learned to your own unique situation.** In this way, each of us can climb our own spiritual ladder – day by day, rung by rung, to maximize this important time on the Jewish calendar so that this year you can truly feel spiritually prepared for Rosh Hashanah and Yom Kippur. That way, you won't just "show up" but instead you'll be ready and able to get that much more from the High Holiday experience.

Although the book is designed to help prepare you for the High Holidays, many of the insights address year-round themes and have timeless lessons: How do we interact with people closest to us? How do we turn stressful experiences into moments of growth? How do we grow spiritually in a material world? What are the practical foundations of Judaism? And of course, how do we express gratitude?

In the spirit of the last question, I would like to thank my

---

*   MJE is a Jewish outreach and educational organization which engages unaffiliated and less affiliated young Jews in Jewish life.
** On Rosh Hashanah, Yom Kippur and on each Shabbat, in order to maintain the sanctity of the day, instead of answering the challenge question in writing, discuss the question with a friend or family member.

esteemed mentor, Rabbi Dr. Jacob J. Schachter, for encouraging me to write this book. Thank you as well to my beloved students at MJE for also inspiring me to write this book. Their curiosity and love of Judaism is the greatest gift that any teacher could hope for. About them our Sages taught, "I learned much wisdom from my teachers and even more from my colleagues. However, from my students I learned most of all" (*Taanit* 7a). Thank you to my publisher, Rabbi Alec Goldstein, of Kodesh Press for being the one to suggest I commit the WhatsApp recordings to a book form. I also wish to thank my colleagues and friends, Rabbi Elly Krimsky, Rabbi Ezra Cohen, and Yoel Saidian, for their insightful and valuable suggestions to give this project added depth and inspiration. Special thanks and gratitude to the MJE supporters who have donated generously to enable this book to come to fruition (see dedication page).

Thank you to my father, Mr. Leon Wildes, for his mentorship, wisdom and love, and to my mother Ruth Wildes, of blessed memory, in whose honor MJE is dedicated. Last, but certainly not least, I wish to thank my wife, Jill, and my children, Yosef, Ezra, Yehuda, and Avigayil, whose love and support have made this book, and everything else I am able to accomplish, possible.

Welcome to *The Forty-Day Challenge*!

Day 1

Second Chances

Rosh Chodesh Elul Day 1

"THE MERCHANT OF DEATH IS DEAD!" THIS WAS REPORTEDLY the headline in the obituary section of a French newspaper in 1888 that erroneously eulogized Alfred Nobel, the Swedish inventor of dynamite. In reality, though, it was Alfred's brother, Ludwig, who had died. Thanks to some poor reporting, the newspaper mistakenly thought Alfred had died, and the reporters published a scathing review of his life. The paper characterized Alfred Nobel as someone who had grown rich by developing new ways to "mutilate and kill." Nobel was deeply impacted by this premature obituary and became obsessed with how he would be remembered. He rewrote his will, bequeathing most of his incredible fortune to a cause that would be admired and celebrated by all: the Nobel Prize that, to this day, is offered to leading scientists, writers, and peace-makers as a way not to harm but to benefit humankind.

The newspaper's historic blunder gave Alfred Nobel the rare opportunity to read his own obituary – it gave Nobel a second chance.

Today begins the Hebrew month of Elul, a month some consider the holiest of the year. What is so special about Elul?

The Jewish Sages teach that God is spiritually closer to us during the month of Elul. We have a tradition that during this time God is more receptive to our prayers and to our attempts to draw closer to His presence (Rashi, Exodus 33:11). The great Chasidic master Rabbi Schneur Zalman of Liadi (1745–1813) uses the metaphor of a king whose usual place is in the palace. Anyone wishing to see the king must first travel to the palace, go through all the gates, and be meticulously prepared. But there are times when the king leaves the palace and comes out to the field to make himself more accessible so that even a simple peasant behind his plow can approach him. Elul is the time when the king, i.e., God, is in the field.

What happened during this period on the Jewish calendar that made Elul such an opportune time for spiritual closeness? The Sages (Rashi, Exodus 33:11) tell us that Rosh Chodesh Elul, the first day of the month, was the day God told Moshe to ascend Mount Sinai *again*, for the second set of tablets.

Let's backtrack a little: Earlier in the summer, we observed a fast day called *Shiva Asar b'Tammuz* or the seventeenth day of the month of Tammuz. That was the day Moshe descended Mount Sinai with the tablets containing the Ten Commandments, only to find the Jewish people worshipping the Golden Calf. It was a terrible moment in Jewish history when the people's faith and relationship with God seemed to be beyond repair. In response, Moshe broke the tablets and remained in the Jewish camp, praying on their behalf, desperately trying to obtain God's forgiveness.

Moshe prayed and beseeched the Almighty for forty days, from the seventeenth of Tammuz – when he first saw the Jews sinning – until Rosh Chodesh Elul. On the first day of Elul, after forty days of pleading for forgiveness, God told Moshe to return to Mount

Sinai. He was ready to give the Jewish people a second chance. Moshe ascended Mount Sinai to receive the *second* set of tablets on this very day.

Elul is all about second chances.

Moshe remained on Mount Sinai for forty more days. He returned to the Jewish encampment with the second set of tablets and guess on what day? It was the tenth day of the Hebrew month of Tishrei, none other than the day of Yom Kippur! Yom Kippur became the Jewish day of atonement because it marked the completion of the process of reconciliation between God and the Jewish people. It represented the culmination of the people's renewed relationship when the Almighty gave them a *second chance* after they had sinned.

God presented a unique challenge to our ancestors during these forty days between Rosh Chodesh Elul and Yom Kippur: fix your problems, deal with your issues, and renew your relationship with Me. Every year at this time, that same forty-day challenge presents itself to us. Like Alfred Nobel, we too are given a *second chance* to confront our challenges, deal with our demons, and reconnect with God and our fellow human beings.

Throughout the year we routinely encounter obstacles and spiritual challenges, which disconnect us from our spiritual source – from God and even from the people we love. We all have dreams and goals we have failed to achieve. We have let ourselves down in some way. But these forty days come to us every year, presenting us with the opportunity to reconnect and draw closer to our unique potential as the new year approaches.

We see this in the very word "Elul," which is spelled *alef, lamed, vav, lamed,* an acronym for a beautiful biblical verse from King Solomon's "Song of Songs," *ani l'dodi v'dodi li,* "I am for my beloved and my beloved is mine" (Song of Songs 6:3). Elul is a month of closeness with our beloved.

"Elul" is also an acronym for another important biblical phrase, *ish l'reyeihu u'matanot l'evyonim*, "one person for his friend and gifts to the poor" (Esther 9:22). This represents another way of spiritually reconnecting during the month of Elul – by helping the less fortunate and being there for our friends.

And so, to take advantage of the power of renewal these next forty days offer us, we will together study forty different Torah ideas and messages – all aimed at helping us grow closer to God and to the most important people in our lives. My suggestion is to take a few minutes each morning to read one new entry and, if possible, set aside another few moments at some other time in the day to *internalize* the idea and answer the challenge question. My hope and prayer is that these spiritual messages will inspire us to confront our challenges and build our character in such a way as to draw closer to God – at a time when He is easier to find. In doing so, may we merit to emerge from this year's Yom Kippur renewed and purified for a sweet and uplifting New Year ahead.

Question: What part of your life deserves a "second chance" – where you can forgive, revisit, or enhance something that will help you become the best version of yourself?

_____

_____

_____

_____

Day 2
Being Honest with Ourselves
Rosh Chodesh Elul Day 2

DR. BEN CARSON BECAME FAMOUS ON THE NATIONAL STAGE
in 2016 when he ran for the Presidency. But by this time, he was
already known as one of the world's leading neuroscientists, having
separated conjoined twins no other doctor could. Despite his
extraordinary medical achievements, Dr. Carson confided that as a
young man, he struggled with anger and rage. At the age of fourteen,
he lunged at his friend with a camping knife. Had the knife not hit
his friend's large belt buckle, he might have killed him. He also
shared how he punched someone, threw rocks, and tried to hit his
own mother with a hammer. Young Ben realized that if he didn't
work on his rage, his life would be over before it began. Through
focused hard work, he learned how to control his fits of anger and
went on to secure a full scholarship to Yale, eventually becoming a
world-famous neurosurgeon.

Ben Carson's recovery all started with being honest with himself.
He was able to admit he had a problem and then went to work on

it. Because he was able to recognize and honestly acknowledge his problem, his life took an entirely different trajectory.

The Torah tells us, "You must not distort judgment and you must not show partiality, and you must not take a bribe" (Deuteronomy 16:19). The Torah then provides us with the reason: "because bribery blinds the eyes of the wise and perverts the words of the just" (Ibid).

Why does the Torah say that bribery "blinds the wise" and "perverts the just"? Why not simply say that bribery has the power to blind people and pervert justice – why does the verse specifically single out people who are "wise" and "just"?

The Torah is teaching us an important lesson. No one is immune from something as alluring as money, not even the wise and just. We *all* possess a good inclination and an evil inclination, and so even the wise and just can succumb to temptation. The Chafetz Chaim and Rebbe Nachman of Breslov – two rabbinic giants who possessed saintly characters – both admitted that by nature they were not easygoing people and shared how hard they had to work to contain their anger. No matter how great we think certain people are, everyone has flaws they struggle to overcome.

The trick is to remain connected to our spiritual source. According to the Talmud, the Hebrew word for a bribe, *shochad*, can be broken up into two words: *shehu chad*, which means "for He is one" (*Ketubot* 105b). Because when a person judges rightly, he becomes a partner with the One – with God Himself. If however one accepts a bribe, he acts alone, but when he resists the temptation and refuses a bribe, the human judge then becomes a partner with the ultimate Judge. When we do the right thing, we become one with our spiritual source, and we are never alone.

And so, as we embark upon this Forty-Day Challenge, trying to work on our flaws and improve our character, we must remember that we *all* have something to work on, even the most righteous and revered sages. What we can learn from the Chafetz Chaim, Rebbe Nachman, and Ben Carson is to be honest with ourselves; to recognize that no matter how great we may think we are, there is a part of us which is attracted to the more material and physical parts of life. But the fact that we have a negative and more base inclination should not distress us. That is simply a part of our spiritual makeup. Acknowledging this reality is critical to positive change.

Being totally honest with ourselves will allow us to better confront the many temptations we all face – be it a bribe to a judge or an anger issue, jealousy, laziness, or greed. If we know that none of us is above temptation, not even the wise or the just, we can approach those situations more realistically.

Question: Is there any area of your life that you are afraid to be honest about? If so, how can you work to go beyond the fear?

_____

_____

_____

_____

Day 3
Finishing What We Start

ON JULY 4, 1976, TERRORISTS HIJACKED AN AIR FRANCE flight from Tel Aviv to Paris and diverted the plane with its 260 passengers to Uganda. The elite forces of the IDF executed a top-secret plan to rescue the hostages led by Jonathan "Yoni" Netanyahu, commander of Israel's elite Sayeret Matkal commando forces. Several giant Hercules transport planes flew from Israel through the night and landed clandestinely in Entebbe Airport in Kampala, Uganda. The IDF soldiers stormed the airport lounge where the Jewish passengers and Air France crew were being held, rescued the passengers, and boarded them safely on the Israeli planes. Israel was jubilant.

But the commander of the troops, Lt. Col. Netanyahu, was shot in the neck during the rescue mission. As the grateful passengers flew north through Africa, they noticed the typically stoic troops weeping, as their beloved commander died on the flight home. It is not known if Yoni was even aware that the mission he planned, and for which he gave his life, had succeeded. Yoni's life was tragically cut short. He did not live to marry his fiancée or to rejoice with his commandos and the freed hostages, nor did he live to see his younger brother, Benjamin, become Israel's longest-serving prime minister. But nobody forgot the sacrifice he made. Thousands of babies were named "Yoni" that year for Israel's newest hero, but the charismatic warrior and poet did not live to see the fruits of his hard work by the time his life was taken at the young age of thirty.

In discussing the laws of warfare, the Torah shares the special exemptions from military service, saying, "What man is there that is fearful and fainthearted? Let him go and return unto his house, lest his brother's heart melt" (Deuteronomy 20:8). A person so filled with fear of battle is exempt from the military since the Torah is concerned that his own fear could diminish the morale of his fellow soldiers.

Besides this exemption, though, the Torah informs us of three other categories of people who are excused from combat: First, someone who has built a home but has not yet lived in it. Second, someone who has planted a vineyard but has not yet redeemed it. Third, a man who became engaged to a woman but has not yet married her (Deuteronomy 20:5–7). The Torah says that each of these three people are exempt from military service, "lest the person die in battle" and then the person who built a home will have to endure another person inaugurating it, the man who planted a vineyard will suffer having another redeem it, and the man who is engaged will have someone else marrying his beloved.

Why are these three individuals singled out? Shouldn't we be concerned with the loss of any human life? If so, why are these three types of people – someone who has built a home but has not yet moved in, someone who has planted a vineyard but not yet redeemed it, and one who is engaged but not yet married – more worthy of a military exemption than anyone else?

Anyone dying in battle is tragic. However, as my friend Rabbi Dr. Ari Berman (President of Yeshiva University) suggested, it is even more distressing to have one's life cut short after working so hard to build something, but before being able to enjoy the fruits of one's labor. War is always awful, but it is even more sorrowful to lose something you have spent a lifetime building, be it a business, home, or relationship.

The Torah wants us to first develop a general sensitivity to human life, but also wants us to further empathize with those who work hard to reach certain life goals, only to have their dreams snatched away before they are realized. Thus we are encouraged to be especially sensitive to someone who loses their job after working crazy hours to secure it in the first place, or another person who spends years building up a business only to see it crumble and fail because of a change in the economy, or someone who – despite working tirelessly on nurturing a romantic relationship – is unable to sustain it for the long run. The Torah is warning us: never underestimate the pain and trauma involved in losing a business or a home, or the difficulty in finding the right match.

As the world continues to struggle with the effects of the COVID-19 pandemic, one does not have to look far to find friends and family who have endured such hardships. What are we doing to be there for them? What have we done or what can we still do to help in a material way to offer a consoling ear? This kind of sensitivity should, of course, be shown all year round but is particularly relevant during the month of Elul.

As we discussed on Day 1 of our Challenge, the word "Elul" is spelled *alef, lamed, vav, lamed,* an acronym for *ani l'dodi v'dodi li,* "I am for my beloved and my beloved is mine" (Song of Songs 6:3). But it is also an acronym for *ish l'reyeihu u'matanot l'evyonim,* "one person for his friend and gifts to the poor" (Esther 9:22). "I am for my beloved and my beloved is mine" symbolizes the relationship we nurture with God during this month, intensifying our prayers and increasing our Torah study. But "one person for his friend and gifts to the poor" teaches us how critical it is to also help our colleagues and those around us during this time, by, digging a bit deeper into our pockets and giving more charity, looking to performing more *chesed*, acts of kindness, to those who truly need it. Giving to others, particularly at this time of year, is not just the right thing to do as we prepare for the High Holiday season, it's the best way to fill our own lives with meaning since we get so much more when we give.

One final thought: When the Torah exempts from military service someone who built a house, planted a vineyard, or got engaged, it is also teaching us the importance of following through on what we have started. We are distressed when we undertake something but do not get to see it through. Conversely, we experience great joy and satisfaction when we commit to something – even something small – and we manage to complete what we began. As we complete Day 3 of our Forty-Day Challenge, let's make sure we continue to learn each day – following through – as we use this time to draw closer to God and our fellow human beings.

Question: Do you have any personal dreams or goals that have been put on pause? Why, and what can you do to get back on track to achieving them?

_____

_____

_____

_____

Day 4
Making Music
with What Remains

THE GREAT VIOLINIST ITZHAK PERLMAN CONTRACTED polio at the age of four, and for his entire life he had to wear metal braces and use crutches to walk. One time, the musician came out on stage, and as he was tuning his violin, one of the strings snapped. Instead of asking for another string, he simply continued to play the whole concert on just three strings (a violin has four strings). When Perlman was finished, the crowd gave him a standing ovation. When they asked him to speak about what happened, he famously remarked, "Our task is to make music with what remains."

As we have discussed, Elul is a time of spiritual closeness: *ani l'dodi v'dodi li*, "I am for my beloved and my beloved is mine," but it is also a time to accept our own reality, to appreciate what we have – even if we don't have all of the strings.

My friend Rabbi Eitan Mayer taught that we can learn a powerful lesson of Elul by reading the word in the reverse. If we spell "Elul" backwards, it reads *lamed, vav, lamed, alef*. This spells *Lulei*, which is a combination of two words: *lu* meaning "if only" and *lo* meaning "no." Thus, *Lulei* literally means "if only, no" – if only things were *not* the way they are. Much of the year, we live a "Lulei" kind of existence where we say to ourselves: "If only things were *not* the way that they are, my life would be so much better."

- *If only* I got a bigger break at work, I would be so much more successful.
- *If only* I were smarter, I would be further along in my career.
- *If only* I were more attractive, people would pay more attention to me.
- *If only* I had different parents, maybe I wouldn't have such problems in my relationships.
- *If only* I had been raised religious, it would so much easier for me to be observant.

If only!

The month of Elul comes along and tells us we've got it *backwards*, because by definition we have exactly what we need to accomplish our goals in life. The great Ramchal – Rabbi Moshe Chaim Luzzatto (eighteenth century) taught that the deck of cards each of us is dealt is presented to us in the specific way it is, in order to challenge our souls in the precise manner we need to grow. The challenges we are given in life are exactly what we need to actualize our unique potential. That is why, although understandable, it is foolish to desire the circumstances of someone else, since they are different than we are and, therefore, need to be placed in a completely different situation to realize their potential.

What is critical to remember is that it is not *what* happens to us in life that is important – that is often out of our control – but rather *how* we react and how we handle the situation. The Talmud teaches us, "Everything is in the hands of Heaven except the fear of Heaven" (*Megillah* 25a). The "fear of Heaven" refers to the values and principles we use to manage the situations in which we find ourselves. *That* we do have control over. So much else – who our parents are, what we look like, or what kind of religious background we come from – are all circumstances over which we have little or no control. But we can control the attitude and values we apply to whatever situations are thrust upon us, and that is ultimately what shapes and develops us into the people we become. The type of person we become does not depend on our circumstances themselves, but rather on how we respond to them. The great psychologist Viktor Frankl said, "Between stimulus and response there is a space. In that space is our power to choose our response. In our response lies our growth and our freedom."

And so, sometimes in life, the string breaks, and we're forced to deal with the situation. Rather than simply becoming upset at the inconvenience, try to visualize your soul needing that difficult moment to get to where it needs to go. In those challenging moments, instead of feeling deprived or playing the "if only" game, let us approach the situation for what it truly is: a growth opportunity. In doing so, we will not only be actualizing our potential but learning to find happiness in what we already have. As the Sages of the Mishnah famously taught: "Who is rich? One who is happy with his portion" (*Chapters of the Fathers* 4:1).

Question: What perceived "weakness" in yourself could you reinterpret as a strength? Alternatively, what setback in your life can you actually use as an advantage?

_____

_____

_____

_____

Day 5
Not by Thought Alone

IN 1644, THE FRENCH PHILOSOPHER RENÉ DESCARTES famously wrote, "I think, therefore I am." Descartes was trying to figure out what it is about human existence that allows us to know we actually exist, but this phrase has also been used by some to describe what makes us human. To be sure, Judaism celebrates the intellect – our ability to think and reason – but the Torah also sees our humanity defined by the development of our character and personality.

The great medieval sage, teacher, and philosopher, Moses Maimonides (twelfth century), wrote a treatise entitled the "Laws of Character Traits" (*Hilchot De'ot*), which focuses on the personality traits that an individual should try to develop and cultivate. And he asks a very simple question: Once a person knows how they want to change and the kind of character modifications he or she would like to make, how should one accustom themselves? What should one do to develop these new personality traits so they can actualize the change they are striving to make?

Maimonides, also known as Rambam, explains, "How can one accustom himself to follow these temperaments to the extent that they become a permanent fixture of his [personality]? He should perform, repeat, and perform a third time, the acts which conform to the standards of the middle of the road temperaments. He should do this constantly, until these acts are easy for him and do not present any difficulty. Then these temperaments will become a fixed part of his personality" ("Laws of Character Traits" 4:7).

Simply put, Rambam is suggesting we engage in the very actions that develop the personality we seek to cultivate and repeat those behaviors a second and third time – a method known as behavioral repetition. For example, if we wish to become a more kind and sensitive person, we should repeatedly perform acts of kindness for other people. Or, if we seek to reverse a negative trait like anger, we should endeavor to control our temper when a situation arises that makes us feel angry inside, continuing to subdue our rage until it no longer feels like a strain and eventually becomes second nature.

To Descartes' statement "I think, therefore I am," Rambam, at least when it comes to personality development, would say, "I *do*, therefore I am." Our actions – not our thoughts – develop us into the people we are. My friend and MJE Israel tour guide Tuvia Book always likes to say, "To do is to Jew" because it's ultimately the actions we take that develop us into the people we become.

One of the most influential Jewish books of all time, the *Sefer Ha-Chinuch* ("The Book of Education") contains this passage: "You must know that a person is influenced by his actions; and his heart and all his thoughts always follow after the actions that he does – whether good or bad. And even he who in his heart is a complete sinner and all the desires of his heart are only for evil; if his spirit shall be enlightened and he will put his efforts and actions to persist in Torah and commandments – even if not for the sake of Heaven – he shall immediately incline towards the good" (Mitzvah #16).

This is the behaviorist approach that was developed in the

twentieth century by psychologists like B.F. Skinner, but its roots stretch far back to our ancient Jewish teachings.

We often think that for our actions to be sincere and genuine, we must always internally desire to do the right thing. In an ideal world, that of course would be true. In reality though, we don't always *feel* like doing the right thing. Yet, Judaism stresses that, irrespective of our feelings, we must strive to *do* the right thing. And that does not make us a hypocrite – just human. Our thoughts aren't always aligned with our actions or behavior, but if we get the behavior right, our thoughts and feelings will follow.

This is why Judaism is mitzvah-centered. Mitzvot are concrete actions we can take. Judaism isn't about simply *thinking* about the right thing – it's about *doing* the right thing. It's about engaging in the right behaviors and taking the correct actions. If we want to feel grateful, then we need to practice gratitude, which Judaism teaches we can do by reciting blessings when we eat or by starting each day with the *Modeh Ani* – a prayer of thanks to God for giving us life. If we want to stop getting angry, we can focus on being calm at times when things get stressful. If we want to improve in any area of life, we take action, repeating the correct behavior again and again. Philosophizing will not lead to change; modifying our behavior will.

We all have our moments. The best time to apply this behaviorist approach is precisely when we're *not* in the mood to do the right thing. We might feel rushed or distracted, we might have other pressing things we need to get done, and we're stressed out; but it is precisely in those moments when we don't *feel* like doing the right thing that we can break out of our negative cycle by *doing* what is correct and right. And don't worry about having the right thoughts and feelings – they'll come after we do the right thing.

Question: What is one act – or mitzvah – that you can start doing anew, even if it *feels* difficult to do so?

_____

_____

_____

_____

Day 6

"Never Sent, Never Signed": Controlling Your Anger

WHENEVER ABRAHAM LINCOLN FELT THE IMPULSE TO TELL someone off, he would compose what he called a "hot letter." He disciplined himself to express his anger by writing a letter, which helped him cool down. Lincoln would then write at the bottom of those letters: "Never sent. Never signed."

Yesterday we learned about Rambam's behaviorist approach to character improvement. Rambam taught that if we want to improve our character or if we want to uproot a negative trait from our personality, we should engage in certain behaviors repeatedly until they become fixed parts of our personality.

Today I'd like to get more specific and focus on the trait of anger. If someone is easily angered, Rambam says one should try to get to a place where things that previously angered him, no longer do so. Generally, Rambam adopts the position that we should follow the golden mean, or the middle path, in all traits. However, in combating anger, he says we should tend toward the extreme: "It is fitting and proper that one move away from [anger] and adopt the opposite extreme. He should train himself not to become angry, even when it is fitting to be angry" ("Laws of Character Traits" 2:3). However, in the previous chapter of the same treatise, he authored on character traits, Rambam says that one *should* get angry over certain things and not be "like a dead person who feels nothing" (Ibid 1:4).

So, according to Rambam, should one ever get angry or not?

The answer suggested by some is that one should endeavor to never feel anger *internally* but to display anger externally when it is necessary to inform or educate. For example, if a student or child acts inappropriately and the teacher or parent does not appear to be upset, the child may mistake their teacher's or parent's lack of reaction as a license to repeat the bad behavior. In those instances, Rambam recommends the parent or teacher display anger externally (in order to educate) but refrain from feeling anger internally. This is certainly a lofty goal but one Rambam believes we should strive toward.

Anger is such a destructive internal force because anger triggers the body's fight-or-flight response, causing the body to release adrenaline and other hormones into the bloodstream. That in turn causes us to think less rationally, which is why we have all probably said or done something foolish in a fit of anger. As Rambam wrote: "Whenever one becomes angry, if he is a wise man, his wisdom leaves him; if he is a prophet, his prophecy leaves him. The life of the irate is not true life" ("Laws of Character Traits" 2:3).

Getting angry on a regular basis has prevented some people from building lasting relationships, establishing careers, and just enjoying life. So, what can we do to prevent ourselves from getting angry?

One simple suggestion is to take a deep breath. Breathing slowly in through the nose and out the mouth actually helps calm us down. Breathing activates our parasympathetic nervous system, which helps the body relax in a stressful situation. It is a simple and useful tool that can be used in any surrounding. "Taking a deep breath takes your focus off whatever's angering you which helps you de-escalate." says Dr. Mitch Abram, a clinical psychologist who assists athletes in working through their anger issues.

The same thing applies to emails, texts, Facebook, and the like. I recently received an email that made me angry, and I instinctively started to type a response, but thankfully I stopped and waited until I could think things out more rationally. I then tweaked the email and sent it out and got a much better response. If we're not sure how our email will be interpreted, it can help to wait an hour, or a day, or show it to a friend before sending it. So much gets lost when we don't have those in-person cues and gestures. Even if the other person sounds confrontational or obnoxious, they may not have meant it that way. And even if they did, that doesn't mean we have to respond in the same way. Remember, once we click or press "send," our tone and message is out there forever. So, take a few breaths, think things through, and don't respond in anger. Or, follow what Lincoln did and write a letter you never sign and never send!

Another suggestion in dealing with anger is getting it off your chest. The Torah tells us "you shall surely correct your neighbor" (Leviticus 19:17), which teaches us to say something when we feel offended or insulted in some way. Nachmanides – the Ramban – in his interpretation of this biblical phrase, wrote that one should specify to the offender what they said or did that was offensive. When we feel that someone has angered or hurt us, but we refrain from expressing our true feelings, that builds up as resentment. There is an appropriate way of sharing our feelings – privately and in a non-confrontational way. I always suggest couching whatever rebuke we may be giving a friend in the language of "When you said this or did that, *it made me feel....*" Focusing the person's behavior on how it made you feel prevents the other person from feeling attacked. That in turn allows your friend to deal with the behavior and not feel he or she has to defend themselves.

Anger is possible to control, and many people we respect greatly have been able to do this. On Day 2 of our Forty-Day Challenge, I shared that the great sage, the Chafetz Chaim, related how he had anger issues. He would sometimes be seen by his students late at night, speaking to himself trying to control his anger. I also mentioned how Rebbe Nachman of Breslov, the great Chasidic master, worked his entire life on anger until he merited to get to a point where virtually nothing angered him.

If we focus on actions that calm us down, wait before sending that next email or text, get things off our chest that bother us, and remember anger is something some great people struggle with but have gotten a handle on, we can subdue our anger and become calmer and happier people.

Question: Which situations generally make you upset or angry? What practical step(s) can you take in order to be calmer in such moments?

_____

_____

_____

_____

Day 7
Achieving Wholeness

Any Torah scholar whose inner self is not like his outer self
is not a Torah scholar.

– Babylonian Talmud, *Yoma* 7b

Sincerity and wholeness of character are imperative for moral
perfection. Rambam, in his treatise of character traits writes: "A
person is forbidden to accustom himself to act in a smooth-tongued
or deceptive manner. He should not speak one thing outwardly and
think otherwise in his heart. Rather, his inner self should be like his
outer self, and what he feels in his heart should be the same as the
words on his lips" ("Laws of Character Traits" 2:6).

Deception can obviously be hurtful and destructive to other people, but it also damages the person doing the deception. Presenting
oneself in a way which is inconsistent with our true selves can create
conflict and turmoil within ourselves, and it prevents us from living
a wholesome type of life.

Rambam continues with a concrete example: "It is forbidden to
deceive people . . . one should not sell non-kosher meat to a gentile
as if it were kosher meat" (Ibid.). We are never permitted to deceive
people by allowing others to think something is true when in

reality it is not. The "used car salesman" has become a cliche about someone who presents the car as perfect when, in fact, there are serious underlying issues. This is called fraud and is something the Torah clearly forbids.

But besides the moral wrong of deception, if we want to develop ourselves spiritually, we need to learn to *be ourselves* and not go through life masquerading as someone else. Always trying to appear morally superior to who we truly are creates inner disharmony and causes problems in our interactions with the most important people in our lives. Relationships must be built on truth – on who we are. Relationships simply don't work when we disguise our true selves, presenting ourselves one way on the outside while feeling different on the inside.

This does not mean that in some situations – like when we are trying to make a good impression on another person – we shouldn't put our best foot forward. If you are on a date or on a job interview, there's nothing wrong with ironing your shirt or dry cleaning your suit, even if you are usually an unkempt person. Rambam isn't precluding these social graces that help us connect or help us make a good impression on others.

What Rambam and the other Jewish sages are teaching is to be honest in our interactions with others and to be careful to not advance ourselves or our relationships through cunning or deceit. In the language of Rambam, it is forbidden "to accustom himself to act in a smooth-tongued or deceptive manner," meaning we should refrain from being one way with our mouths and another in our hearts.

Everybody loves being around people who seem to be sharing who they truly are, where, as they say, "what you see is what you get." We can generally tell when someone is trying to be something they're not, and it's usually a turn-off. We can also somehow naturally sense when someone is being sincere and genuine, and that is always attractive. As we finish the first full week of our Forty-Day Challenge, let us strive to live as the well-known Hebrew phrase goes: *tocho k'boro* – where the way we act on the outside mirrors who we are on the inside.

Question: What is one time when you acted one way but felt another way inside? When this or a similar situation arises in the future, how can you go about being *tocho k'boro* – where your outside actions mirror your inner feelings?

_____

_____

_____

_____

Day 8
Smile

Smile, though your heart is aching
Smile, even though it's breaking
When there are clouds in the sky
you'll get by ... If you'll just smile

This song, made famous by Nat King Cole, teaches the power of smiling, even when we're not feeling like it.

Yesterday we spoke of the value in being authentic, sincere, and whole – where our outsides mirror our insides. Today I'd like to share the power of doing something positive on the outside so that we can feel better on the inside.

Rambam, again in his "Laws of Character Traits," writes: "One should neither be excessively laughing and joking and not sad or mournful – rather he should be happy" (2:7). The Rambam teaches us not to feel dejected, walking around like the weight of the world is on our shoulders, and at the same time, to take life seriously and not reduce everything to a joke.

Rambam advocated following the Greek philosopher Aristotle's belief in the Golden Mean, namely, that one should always strive to follow the middle path. In this case, the middle path between frivolity and depression is *simcha*, which means "happiness." Rambam continues by saying, "One should greet everyone in a cheerful manner" (Ibid.). This is a direct quote from the *Ethics of the Fathers* (4:14), which teaches that we should receive everyone with a positive countenance. Thus, a person should strive to act toward others *b'simcha*, in joy, but not a fake type of joy where one smiles and laughs at everything, pretending that everything is always wonderful. We know that in real life there are struggles, so if someone always says things are amazing, we know they're being insincere. At the same time, Rambam is teaching us that we should also refrain from becoming despondent and instead greet people with a smile.

However, does this not contradict what we studied yesterday? Rambam taught that what one feels in their heart should be the same as the words on their lips (Ibid. 2:6) – that our outsides should mirror our insides. And yet here, Rambam is telling us that we should be cheerful and upbeat even when we don't feel like it! What if we're feeling sad or even depressed when we meet someone? Wouldn't acting in a cheerful manner be insincere and perhaps even deceitful?

I believe Rambam is reminding us of something we learned a few days ago – that our internal thoughts and feelings often follow the actions we take: "After one's actions follow one's heart" (*Sefer Ha-Chinuch*). If we want to improve the way we're feeling *internally*, then we must act *externally* in a way which is positive and upbeat. Acting this way on the outside, at least temporarily, can help us feel better on the inside. Studies show that smiling can literally trick our brains into feeling happy, by releasing chemicals like dopamine and serotonin. It's a shortcut we can use to feel better about ourselves and about others too. Because when we smile, people around us feel better and react to us more favorably. And everyone wants to be around someone who is positive.

This is especially true in marriage. Leading professor of psychology, Dr. David Pelcovitz, observes that the first and last thirty seconds one talks to their spouse can color the rest of the conversation. If we come home from work annoyed or cranky – and we begin the interaction with our spouse in a negative way – then the whole evening can be stressful. However, if we smile when we return home and we start with a kind word, the rest of the evening will often proceed more successfully, even if we're a little stressed out. Maybe we can share our anxieties once we get settled in, but it's critical to first establish a positive connection. The same is true when we leave for work in the morning. If we just mumble "goodbye" because we're already focused on a work project we're behind on, then we lose that moment of connection before being away for hours. Greeting everyone positively isn't just for the stranger on the street (though that's important too), but for the most important people in our lives.

There will always be times that we experience sadness, or we feel like we have the weight of the world upon our shoulders. When we feel this way, let's remember Rambam's teaching to make a small change on the outside so we can feel more positive inside. If we make the effort to smile – even when we're not feeling that way – the people around us will also smile and respond more favorably to us, and we can feel stronger in our relationships. Smiling, or any positive gesture or comments for that matter, triggers happiness within ourselves. So smile!

Question: Do you know someone who is, right now, in need of support and inspiration? What small step(s) can you take to help make them smile?

_____

_____

_____

_____

Day 9
The Real You

DURING THE HOLOCAUST, TENS OF THOUSANDS OF DIS-
traught Jewish parents, seeing the fateful writing on the wall, depos-
ited their small children with Christian neighbors and even local
churches, in the hope that their children would survive the war.
Tragically, most of these parents were murdered by the Nazis. In 1945,
after the war was over, Rabbi Eliezer Silver of the United States and
Dayan Isidor Grunfeld of the United Kingdom were dispatched as
military chaplains to Europe to rescue these children. Rabbis Silver
and Grunfeld approached the priests who ran a monastery in Alsace-
Lorraine, France, asking for the Jewish orphans to be transferred
to their next of kin. The priests insisted documentation would be
needed to identify the Jewish children. When the rabbis were able
to identify children with Jewish surnames, the priests said that last
names could not prove the children's Jewishness. The rabbis asked
if they could return that night, and the priests reluctantly agreed.
The two spiritual leaders arrived as the children were in their beds,
about to go to sleep for the night. The rabbis walked through the
room of children and began to sing the *Shema* – the declaration of

faith that Jewish children learn at a very young age. Immediately, the little children began to cry out "Mommy, *Mamushka, maman…*"

Based on these responses, the rabbis were able to identify the Jewish children and return them to their relatives.

Hearing the *Shema* brought these children back to their earliest memories with their mothers. Deep down, perhaps even subconsciously, these Jewish orphans, left only with fleeting memories of their beloved parents, understood who they were at their core. When they heard the call of *Shema*, their souls responded.

Who are we, really? Deep down, existentially and metaphysically, what are we made of?

The Torah tells us, "When you are reaping the harvest in your field, and you forget a bundle in the field, you shall not go again to get it; it shall be for the convert, for the orphan, and for the widow, so that the Lord your God will bless you in all the work of your hands" (Deuteronomy 24:19).

The Torah is telling us that if someone accidentally leaves a bundle of grain in the field and forgets to harvest it, God will give that person a great blessing. The Lubavitcher Rebbe, Rabbi Menachem Mendel Schneerson (twentieth century), asked the obvious question: why should a person receive a blessing for doing something accidentally or unwittingly? If by accident I happen to drop some money on the floor and a poor person finds it and is able to use it, did I really do a mitzvah? I didn't intend to give *tzedakah* (charity), and if I didn't even try to do anything good, why should I be rewarded? And so, if a farmer accidentally leaves a pile of grain in the field and a poor person eats it, why does the Torah say God will give the farmer a special blessing?

The Lubavitcher Rebbe explains that if someone performs a mitzvah, even if it was not consciously intended, it is nonetheless consistent with one's internal subconscious desire to do that mitzvah – in this case, the desire to give that *tzedakah*. This is based on a beautiful idea found in Jewish thought that deep down – existentially and metaphysically – we are people who want to do God's will. Sometimes the *yetzer hara* (evil inclination) gets involved and helps us intellectualize or rationalize away our inappropriate behavior – but that's not who we really are. Deep down, we are individuals who *want* to do the right thing. That's why we feel good when we do a mitzvah – when we do something we know is commanded by the Torah. When we attend synagogue or pray at home, even if the experience isn't the most inspiring, it still makes us feel good, as we do when we help out a stranger in need by giving them *tzedakah* or when we take the time to help a friend by giving some needed advice or just lending a listening ear. Even if performing a certain mitzvah doesn't quite inspire us, since we know we're doing the right thing, it makes us feel good because that's who we really are.

That is why Rambam rules that "One may hit a man until he finally says: 'I want to give my wife a divorce writ'" ("Laws of Divorce" 2:20). If a marriage has broken down beyond repair and the man refuses to give his wife a "get" – a religious writ of divorce (which is necessary to dissolve the marriage) – Jewish law says that we can push or strike him until he agrees to divorce her. Today we have other ways to deal with recalcitrant husbands, but at least in theory this is a valid way to end a marriage that is irreconcilable. But isn't this a form of coercion? In Jewish law, like most legal systems, if someone is coerced into doing something, his actions do not have legal validity. Why, then, do we say that if we physically assault someone to the point that he finally agrees to divorce his wife, the *get* is valid? The divorce writ would be null and void since it was coerced!

However, the belief is that by striking the man in this situation, we are simply helping him do what he already wants to do. As

Rambam writes, "He wants to be part of the Jewish people, and he wants to perform all the commandments and he wants to distance himself from all sins. It is only his evil inclination that impels him [to do the wrong thing]" (Ibid.). Right now, the husband is being spiteful and acting in a terribly cruel manner, causing his wife unnecessary anguish. But that's not who he really is. That is why pushing or hitting the husband to give his wife a *get* is not coercion. It is just helping the husband reign in his evil inclination, which is preventing him from doing the right thing – what he really wants to do. Jewish law is founded on the idea that even when we act selfishly or in a mean way, deep down, in our essence, we desire to do what's right.

So, if a person drops money that a poor person finds, the "donor" has performed an action which is consistent with his true nature and inner desire to fulfill God's word. He therefore receives a blessing from God.

This is both a beautiful and important way to look at ourselves. Yes, we have a *yetzer hara* and so we have issues and problems and we sometimes don't do the right thing – but that is not who we are. Deep down, metaphysically, we want to follow the Torah. We want to pray and study Torah, and we want to give *tzedakah*. And so, when the farmer forgets his bundle during harvest time, there is a part of him saying, "I want to leave this for the poor. I want to do the right thing. I want to be closer to God."

That is who we really are.

Question: What mitzvah do you currently perform that makes you feel connected to the deepest part of yourself? How can you enhance your performance of that mitzvah?

_____

_____

_____

_____

Day 10
What Are Your Priorities?

MANY HAVE THE CUSTOM OF STAYING UP ALL NIGHT STUDY-ing Torah on the first night of the festival of Shavuot, which celebrates the giving of the Torah at Sinai. This honored custom came about as a result of a certain failing by the Jewish people. After witnessing the miraculous Ten Plagues and the splitting of the Red Sea, the Jews should have eagerly and excitedly anticipated the Revelation at Sinai, which took place just a few weeks later. But tradition has it that on the morning of the giving of the Torah, the nation needed to be awakened. They were sleeping! Instead of staying up to spiritually prepare themselves for this once-in-a-lifetime encounter with God, the Jews slept the morning away. As a result, Jews to this day stay up all night studying Torah on Shavuot to atone and rectify for their lack of anticipation.

If in college we pulled an all-nighter preparing for a final exam, or we stay up on New Year's Eve to watch the ball drop, it shows we are capable of extending ourselves when we want to. On Black Friday every year, I marvel at how early people get up or how long they are willing to wait in line just to save a few dollars on their new flat-screen TVs.

Life boils down to priorities. We have limits to our time and to our energies. We therefore have to decide how and where we're going to allocate our precious resources. What are we willing to stay up late at night for? What are we willing to wait in line for? The month of Elul is the time we determine where our priorities lie and where and to what causes we dedicate ourselves.

The Torah tells us, "An Ammonite or Moabite shall not enter into the congregation of the Lord; even to their tenth generation they shall not enter into the congregation of the Lord forever" (Deuteronomy 23:4). We are never allowed to accept anyone from the Ammonite or Moabite tribes (which, incidentally no longer exist) as converts. Why is this so?

The Torah gives two reasons. First the Torah says, "Because they did not greet you with bread and with water on the way, when you came forth out of Egypt" (Ibid. 4). After hundreds of years of slavery, when the Jewish people were passing their territory in the wilderness, the Ammonites and Moabites failed to greet the recently emancipated Jewish people with offerings of bread or water.

The Torah gives a second reason: "and because they hired against you Bilaam...to curse you" (Ibid.). Bilaam was the non-Jewish prophet who, according to the Jewish Sages, had prophetic powers that rivaled even Moshe. Unlike Moshe, though, Bilaam sold his prophetic talents to the highest bidder. When the Moabites wanted to curse the Jews, they hired Bilaam for the task, and if not for God's direct intervention, the Jewish people would have been annihilated.

For these two reasons, the Jewish people are not permitted to accept a convert nor marry anyone descended from these two nations – for all eternity.

The first reason, however, does not seem to justify this strict treatment. It is certainly not a good thing to abstain from helping a downtrodden people, but it's also a huge proposition to feed an entire nation – millions of recently freed slaves. Maybe the Ammonites and Moabites didn't have the resources available. Or, even if they did, withholding bread and water does not seem to be enough of a crime to justify the penalty. Also, compared to the second reason the Torah gives – that they hired Bilaam to actively curse the Jewish people with destruction – not giving bread and water doesn't seem so bad! If cursing the Jews is so much worse than not providing food, then why does the Torah need to list both reasons? It's a little like saying someone should go to jail for running a red light and also for committing murder. One infraction is so much worse than the other – why even mention the red light? So why does the Torah need to tell us both reasons – not being hospitable (passive, minor infraction) and cursing (active desire to harm)?

The Dubno Maggid (eighteenth century) says that it's really only one reason. When the Torah informs us of the first reason – that Ammon and Moab did not come with food and drink when the Jews left Egypt – maybe you can give them the benefit of the doubt and say they lacked the financial resources to feed an entire nation. But then when the Torah gives the second reason – because they hired Bilaam to curse the Jewish people – then we know they had the resources to help. That is because we know how much money they were prepared to pay Bilaam to curse the Jews. Ammon and Moab paid Bilaam a huge sum of money. They basically gave him a blank check and let him fill it in. They wanted the Jews gone, whatever the price. For this, they had money. For this, they were prepared to spend their precious resources, but not to supply a nation of former slaves with some food and water.

The message is clear. We must decide how to best use our precious resources. Elul is a time when we evaluate our priorities, when we decide how to allocate our time, our money, and our emotional energy. Where are we going to direct our scarce resources? Are we going to use them to bring other people down – like Ammon and Moab – or will we use our blessings and resources to elevate the people around us – and ourselves in the process? No matter how much money or free time we have, by definition, there is always a limit. If you spend ten dollars in one place, it cannot be spent in another. If you invest five minutes on one project, that's five minutes less for another. Elul is our time to get our priorities properly aligned so we can spend our limited resources in the best possible way: quality time with the people who matter, and investing in our relationship with God, Torah and mitzvot.

Question: What change(s) can you make to better prioritize how you spend your time and your money in order that these gifts can be more directed toward your moral and spiritual well-being?

_____

_____

_____

_____

Day 11
Learning from Our Enemies

RIGHT AFTER THE JEWS LEFT EGYPT, THE NATION OF Amalek launched a sneak attack from behind. They targeted the most vulnerable – the elderly and the children. The Torah explains, "Remember what Amalek did unto you by the way, when you came forth out of Egypt. How they met you on the road and attacked those behind you, and even those that were feeble behind you, when you were faint and weary; and they did not fear God" (Deuteronomy 25:17–18).

It is no coincidence that in synagogue we read about Amalek's attack in the month of Elul. The Torah uses a unique Hebrew phrase to refer to what Amalek did to the Jewish people: *asher karcha ba-derech* which literally means, "they met you on the way." However, the Hebrew word *karcha* is also related to the word *kar*, which means "cool down." (A *mekarer* is a refrigerator.)

What does it mean that Amalek *cooled down* the Jewish people? When the Jews left Egypt, they were on a spiritual high. They had just escaped the most powerful civilization in the world and watched their oppressors brought to their knees. They witnessed the wonders of the Ten Plagues and experienced the miraculous splitting of the

Red Sea, after which they broke out into spontaneous song: "This is my God and I will glorify Him, the God of my father and I will exalt Him" (Exodus 15:2).

The Jews upon leaving Egypt were passionate and enthusiastic about their relationship with God. And to the rest of the nations, they also came to represent the power of God. After all, look what miracles God did for them! And so, the Jews were untouchable. Nobody would dare start with them, for fear of angering their all-powerful and protective God.

And then Amalek came along and cooled everyone down. They took on the Jewish people and in doing so, provoked God Himself. As a result of this ambush, the nations of the world lost their fear, and the Jews lost some of their religious fervor. Their passion was cooled.

Amalek's confrontation also opened up the possibility for other nations to attack the Jews. They showed that if you can find their weak spot, the Jews were not impervious to assault. Rashi, the great medieval commentator, compared Amalek's attack to jumping into a boiling hot bathtub. At first, nobody would dare jump into a boiling tub for fear of getting burned, but as soon as one person has the nerve to do so, he cools it down for the rest to jump in. Amalek is considered the greatest enemy of the Jewish people because they didn't just attack, they paved the way for others to do the same.

Amalek's ambush cooled things down, both for the nations of the world and for the Jews themselves. Their assault chilled the Jewish people's excitement and passion for their new God, whose love for them had seemed so apparent. There are always things that "cool down" our relationship with God, events and circumstances that interfere with our ability to see God in the world and prevent us from feeling His presence in our everyday lives. Amalek isn't just some ancient tribe who attacked our ancestors thousands of years ago. Amalek is that force that, to this day, weakens our enthusiasm for God and replaces it with something lukewarm and tepid. Elul is our time to regain that excitement. It's our time each year, as we approach the High Holiday season, to remember how much of a force God is in our lives, and it is our time to rededicate ourselves to His holy Torah.

One more important teaching on Amalek: Rashi tells us that the word *karcha* is also related to the word *mikreh*, which means "happenstance" or "coincidence." Amalek also comes to represent the idea that things in life are random, that the world and life itself just happens on its own without any guiding force – for no rhyme or reason. There is no plan for our existence. We just happen to be here.

If Judaism stands for anything, it is that *everything* happens for a reason. There *is* a plan, and therefore, whatever does occur in this world has meaning and purpose and is meant to teach us something or designed to enable us to grow in some way.

Learning from our enemies is an important thing. Elul is therefore a good time to think about Amalek and the two lessons we can learn from our encounter with them: first, when we feel passionate about our relationship with God, be wary of those forces that may "cool you down"; and second, remember life is not random. Whatever happens to us, happens for a reason and is meant to learn and grow from.

Question: What challenging situation in your life or bad habits "cool you down" and prevent you from reaching your life goals? Identify two specific ways to better navigate the situation or break the bad habit.

_____

_____

_____

_____

Day 12
Love Thy Neighbor

DURING THIS MONTH OF ELUL, WHEN WE ARE FOCUSED ON growing ourselves, connecting to God, and improving our relationships with our fellow human beings, we think of the central phrase in the Torah governing our relationships with other people: "Love your neighbor as yourself" (Leviticus 19:18). According to the great sage of the Talmud, Rabbi Akiva, this verse represents the most important principle in the Torah (Jerusalem Talmud, *Nedarim* 9:4).

I always struggled with this commandment. Is it possible for us to love someone else as much as we love ourselves? Can we really be expected to show the same level of love and consideration to others as we would to ourselves? The *Rishonim*, the medieval rabbinic commentaries, struggle with this question, and most of these sages do not believe this verse should be read literally. Some suggest the verse means putting yourself in other people's shoes – asking yourself what you would want if you yourself were in your friend's situation. If, for example, a friend fell ill, "love your neighbor as yourself" would mean asking yourself what you would want if you were sick and then doing those very things for your friend. So, if you would want other people to pray for you or visit you, then praying and visiting your friend would be the way to fulfill this commandment. But it doesn't literally mean loving another person as yourself because that is just an impossibility. That is the opinion of most of the Rishonim.

However, Rambam understands "love your neighbor as yourself" literally. He explains the verse in the following manner: "I should have mercy for and love my brother as faithfully as I love and have mercy for myself. This applies to his financial and physical state, and whatever he has or desires. What I want for myself I should want for him, and whatever I don't want for myself or my friends, I shouldn't want for him" (*Book of Commandments*, Positive Commandment #206). Rabbi Moshe Chaim Luzzatto, in his classic book *The Path of the Just*, writes even more strongly, "'as yourself' – with no difference whatsoever, 'as yourself' – without distinction, without devices and schemes, literally 'as yourself'" (ch. 11).

How are we to understand Rambam's opinion that this verse should be read and applied literally? Rabbi Richard Mann, one of my teachers, suggested that the answer is in the continuation of the verse: "you shall love your neighbor as yourself; I am God." The verse doesn't end with "yourself," but with "God." This verse is found in the middle of the book of Leviticus, and we've already been introduced to God many times in the Torah. Why do we need to be told "I am God" after the commandment to "love your neighbor"?

There's a basic principle in modern psychology that we cannot love anyone else unless we first love ourselves. The Torah seems to endorse this idea since the verse says "love your neighbor *as yourself*" – implying you already love yourself. But what aspect of ourselves does God want us to love? How we look? How much money we make? How popular we are? These aspects of our lives may seem important, but they do not define the essence of who we are as humans.

The phrase "I am God" follows "love thy neighbor as yourself" to teach us that it's the part of us that is godly that we are supposed to love, namely our souls. If we develop and cultivate a love for that part of us – for our souls – the part of us that is connected to God, then we can love other people since they too are created in God's image with a soul. The soul is ultimately what connects us all to each other, Our different languages, different cultures, and different countries, separate us, but the godly soul is what unites us. And so, if the soul is the part of you which you have come to love, then you can love others also created with a soul.

When we see another person walking down the street, since they look and sound so different from us, we feel totally disconnected. Remember, they too are created in God's image with a holy soul. And if we have successfully cultivated a love for our own souls, what's to stop us from loving theirs?

Question: Identify someone who is very different from you politically or ideologically. What do you know about them that still makes them worthy of your love? Also, how can you show them, that despite your differences, you respect and care for them?

_____

_____

_____

_____

Day 13
Consistency

WHAT IS THE MOST IMPORTANT VERSE IN THE ENTIRE
Torah?

The medieval Jewish composition called the *Ein Yaakov* quotes
three different answers. According to one sage, Rabbi Akiva, the
most important verse in the Torah is the famous – "love your neighbor as yourself" (Leviticus 19:18; see Jerusalem Talmud, *Nedarim*
9:4). Another sage, Ben Zoma, says the most important verse is,
"Hear O Israel, the Lord is our God, the Lord is one" (Deuteronomy
6:4) – the *Shema* prayer we say daily to express our belief in one
God.

A third rabbi, Shimon ben Pazzi, suggests an obscure and seem-
ingly mundane verse – "You shall offer one lamb in the morning, and
the other lamb you shall offer in the afternoon" (Numbers 28:4). At
first glance, this verse seems pretty bland and uninspiring. It refers
to the daily obligation to sacrifice one lamb in the morning and one
in the afternoon as part of the regular offering in the Jewish Temple.
We can understand how loving one's neighbor and believing in God
are central to our lives as Jews, but what is so important about the
daily sacrificial rite?

Belief in God and concern for one's fellow human beings are groundbreaking ideas that have changed the world. But there's another fundamental concept which Judaism can also take pride in bringing to the fore: consistency – the value in sticking with something *every day*. In the days of the Temple, the same offering was brought every single day. On Shabbat and the holidays new offerings were added, but no matter the day, the Temple service always started with the same lamb in the morning and another one in the afternoon. It may not always be exciting to do the same thing day after day, but that is precisely how we accomplish the changes we want to see in our lives.

Professional athletes will tell you that the best way to get into shape is to have a routine which you must stick to – every day. That's also how we build spiritual muscle when it comes to our relationship with God, and it is no different with our friends or spouses. In relationships, you can't show up some days and be absent other times. Love and trust cannot be developed in a haphazard fashion. They need to be consistent if they are to be meaningful.

That is why when it comes to prayer, ideally – we should set aside time to pray the entire morning service every day. If we are not in that place religiously, we can simply recite the Morning Blessings (*birkot ha-shachar*) – the blessings we say each morning to thank God for those things in life we take for granted: our sight, our clothing, our ability to walk, and even our ability to stretch out our bodies. It takes but a few moments to recite these blessings, but the power of starting our day by expressing gratitude is immense. And doing it *every day* makes all the difference.

If we are starting to observe Shabbat – again, even if it isn't the whole thing, we try to make it consistent. Whatever the Shabbat mitzvah is, be it lighting candles or attending Shabbat services, we try to make sure to do it every week. Whatever we do to connect to God and to be better people, consistency is the key. Like with working out, the routine of the everyday creates muscle memory. That muscle memory is an excellent device to combat the sluggishness that inevitably sets in and which often keeps us from achieving our goals. If we stop working out when we get tired, we won't see progress. The results come about only after we push through – even if we're a little tired or sore. That's how we become great, by doing whatever it is we want to become *every day*. That's when change is actualized.

Belief in God is critical, as is loving your neighbor, but without daily and consistent activities that connect us to God and which benefit our neighbors, these lofty ideas, will remain just that – ideas. "You shall offer one lamb in the morning, and the other lamb you shall offer in the afternoon" (Ibid.). To transform ideas into reality, consistency is the name of the game.

Question: List one spiritual practice (prayer, Torah study, giving charity, visiting the sick) and one general activity (exercise, painting, writing) that bring you joy and fulfillment. How can you make these practices more consistent in your life?

_____

_____

_____

_____

Day 14

If You See Something, Say Something

HOW DO WE HANDLE SITUATIONS IN WHICH WE ARE EMBAR-
rassed or offended?

The Torah teaches: "You shall not hate your brother in your heart,
you shall surely correct your neighbor, and you shall not bear sin
on his account" (Leviticus 19:17).

The verse contains three separate phrases: The first phrase – "You
shall not hate your brother in your heart" – teaches the Torah prohibition to hate a fellow Jew. The second clause – "you shall surely
correct your neighbor" – informs us of the mitzvah to correct one's
neighbor when he or she acts inappropriately. The third and final
phrase – "and you shall not bear sin on his account" is somewhat
elusive. What sin is this referring to and how are all of these three
clauses, found in this one verse, related to one another?

The great medieval commentator Nachmanides (Ramban, thir-
teenth century) teaches that these three clauses – not hating, correcting one's neighbor, and not bearing sin – are all interconnected.
The verse, says the Ramban, is referring to a situation in which one

person has offended another. In such a case, the Torah instructs the offended party to "correct [their] neighbor" by speaking up and asking the offender: "Why have you done such and such to me?" The Torah commands the offended person to express their feelings of hurt, and the Ramban believes that failure to call out the inappropriate behavior will result in the offended party "bearing sin because of him" – what sin? The sin of hating your brother in your heart.

The best way to prevent a person from developing hate in their heart, after they have been insulted or slighted, is for them to speak up and get it off their chest. The Torah wants us to pull the person aside and share our true feelings, rather than bottling up our emotions. This is the mitzvah of *tochachah* – giving reproof or "correcting" one's fellow – and it is done, says the Ramban, to prevent us from violating the Torah's prohibition of hating a fellow Jew.

I don't believe Nachmanides is teaching that we should *always* say something when we're upset. If what is offending you turns out to be something trivial, then try to let it go, but if you are offended – then don't sweep it under the rug. Say something. Do it privately, and try to be as non-confrontational as possible, but say something. Politely explain why you were offended and try to be strategic with the words you use.

It is precisely when we are upset that we must be even more careful with our choice of words. When correcting our neighbor, or what the rabbis call "giving rebuke," we need to think about how the other person will receive our words. What will it be like for the other person to hear what we are about to say? It may temporarily make us feel better to speak in a condescending or harsh tone, but if the point is to be heard and ultimately reconcile the relationship, the less confrontational the tone the better.

This is even more true in close relationships. Dr. John Gottman, one of America's most important researchers in the field of psychology, coined the term "harsh startup." He gives the example of a wife who makes a simple request of her husband, "Please take out the garbage." But the husband doesn't do it. The wife is obviously justified in being upset. But even when we're upset, we have a choice. We might say, "You never do anything. I have to do all of the housework." This is what Dr. Gottman calls a harsh startup. It immediately makes the other person defensive or even combative in their response.

What should we do instead? Avoid "you" statements like "*you* never listen" or "*you* never do anything I ask." Instead, use "I" statements: "*I* don't like when you don't take out the garbage," or "*I* feel like you don't value me when you forget to do what I ask." Using language such as, "Here's how *I felt* when you did that" creates a spirit of cooperation and goodwill. It encourages openness and communication, and it prevents the other person from getting defensive. Accusing the person is simply counterproductive because our goal is to get the other person to recognize how their actions hurt us and make them comfortable enough to apologize.

As you can see, "correcting" or "giving rebuke" is an art form and something which requires great tact, sensitivity, and training.

The same holds true when we see a fellow Jew violating a religious principle. Judaism teaches that since one Jew is responsible for another, if we see a fellow Jew doing something against the Torah, the above quoted biblical phrase – "you shall surely correct your neighbor" – teaches us to say something. But we should only speak up if we reasonably think our words can make a positive difference. If you don't think your intervention or comment will be favorably received, then there is no mitzvah to say anything. If, however, we can share something positive about a certain mitzvah, and in doing so encourage our fellow Jew to observe it – then the Torah wishes us to do so. Again, it is advisable to use positive language such as: "here is something that has helped me in the past" or "this mitzvah contains great wisdom and has brought me joy and meaning." If this comment or suggestion comes across as an expression of care and love – the only proper motivation to say something – it is more likely to be well received.

If we can train ourselves in the art of "correcting our neighbor," we will not only be helping our neighbors become better friends and Jews – we will also move our most important relationships to a higher level.

Question: Is there someone in your life – a friend, colleague, or relative – who has offended you or hurt you in some way? Write down what you would like to say to this person to politely express why you are upset. What else would it take for you to heal and start that relationship anew?

_____

_____

_____

_____

Day 15
The Psychology of Gossip

Great minds discuss ideas; average minds discuss events;
small minds discuss people.

– Eleanor Roosevelt

SEVERAL DAYS AGO, WE DISCUSSED ONE OF THE MOST
important positive commandments in regard to our fellow man –
the mitzvah of "loving one's neighbor as oneself." Today I'd like to
focus on the critical negative commandment vis-à-vis our fellow
human beings – the prohibition of *lashon hara* – speaking ill of
others.

According to Jewish tradition, there are three categories of slander. In increasing severity, they are: *Rechilut* (tale-bearing), *Lashon
Hara* (speaking ill of others), and *Motzi Shem Ra* (defamation).

Rechilut – tale-bearing or gossip derives from the biblical prohibition, "You shall not go around as a tale-bearer among your people"
(Leviticus 19:16). These statements involve private information
about other individuals but they aren't necessarily negative or false
and so they appear totally innocent. One example is the statement,
"Did you hear so-and-so spent $100,000 to renovate their kitchen?"
It's not negative information nor is it false. Still the Torah does

not wish us to discuss the details of someone else's life or become fixated on how others spend their time or money, especially if that information can lead others to become jealous.

Lashon hara, which literally means "evil speech," involves sharing negative information about another person – even if the information is true. There's a common misconception that if the information is true, it is then permissible to share with others. This may be the case under American law, which asserts truth as a defense against slander, but that's not the way Judaism views the matter. Since the negative communication, albeit truthful, still harms the person about whom it is spoken, the Torah prohibits such language. The main exception to this rule is if that information is somehow necessary for the listener to know about. Two common examples include business and matchmaking. If, for example, you have first-hand knowledge of a colleague's fraudulent dealings, and your friend is about to hire this person for their company, you can and must share your knowledge. To be clear though, your knowledge of the fraud must be first-hand and not merely rumored or hearsay. The same criterion applies to the realm of matchmaking. In general, though, if the negative speech serves no immediate and practical purpose, then it is prohibited.

The third and worst category is *Motzi Shem Ra*, which literally means "bringing out a bad name" (see Deuteronomy 22:14). This is the prohibition of defamation, which refers to information which is both negative and false and will cause damage to a person's reputation. Jewish law considers defamation actionable, requiring the defamer to pay a monetary fine.

The common thread running through all three forms of slander – gossip, evil speech, and defamation – is the focus we have on other people's lives. Why does it feel so good to speak or hear about the details of other people's lives? Why do the tabloids, gossip columns, and celebrity news have such a fixation on what a famous person did on a particular day?

This really begs a larger question: From where do we derive our sense of self? If our sense of self is rooted in realizing our own potential, then we will always be looking *up* to God, not *around* to other people. If, however we look at ourselves relative to how *other* people are doing, then the focus shifts from ourselves to others and the likelihood of gossip becomes much greater.

This can help us understand a curious statement found in the Talmud that someone who gossips is likened to someone who worships idols (see *Erchin* 15b). This seems like a radical assertion. While both gossip and idolatry are prohibited, what is the relationship between worshipping idols and gossip?

There are two ways of feeling better about ourselves: developing our own God-given potential or comparing our lives to other people and feeling as though we are doing "better" than others. The former requires discipline and effort, but the latter is much simpler. If we can convince ourselves we that are superior to others, we can feel better about our lives without having to put in the hard work to reach our potential. It's a quick fix. Yet it betrays the fact that our sense of self is not coming from how far we've actually advanced ourselves, but rather on how we are doing in relation to others. In a sense, it is a form of worshipping other people, since we gauge our success relative to other *people* and not in regard to our potential given by *God*. If we operate from this people-obsessed type of existence, then speaking ill of others will, no doubt, make us feel better, Our self-worth will be based on how we fare in relation to other people. The worse others seem to be doing, the better we will feel. This is why gossiping feels so good. It feeds the smallest part of who we are and creates a smokescreen of success keeping us from doing the real work to reach our potential.

Thus, speaking ill of others harms the people about whom we speak, causing irreparable damage to the reputation of friends and colleagues. Gossip and slander also create a false sense of growth within the speaker of *lashon hara*, allowing the gossiper to feel good about themselves without doing the hard work necessary to improve. So, as we continue to advance spiritually during this month of Elul, let us be extra mindful about how we speak about others. Before making that comment or sharing that story, let us think about the impact it will have – not only on the other person, but also on ourselves.

Question: List one or two scenarios in your daily life that expose you to gossip. How can you limit those activities or somehow prevent the gossip or slander from taking place?

_____

_____

_____

_____

Day 16
Holy Grapes

MANY YEARS AGO, I WAS VISITING MY FRIEND ARI AFTER he made *Aliyah* – after he had just emigrated to Israel. He settled with his family in Chashmonaim, a suburban community outside of Jerusalem. We were talking in his backyard while my children were playing on the swings. Beside the swings, he had the most exquisite plants and trees as well as a small vineyard whose luscious grapes looked very appetizing. I plucked a grape off the vine and as I was about to pop it into my mouth, Ari stopped me.

"Mark," he said, "this is Israel. The ground here is holy. You can't just snatch up a grape and eat it!" He went on to explain that parts of the grapes or any fruit grown in Israel belong to the Kohen (Jewish Priest), the Levi (Levite) and the poor, based on the Torah's laws of *trumah* and *ma'aser* (tithing). "Those grapes," Ari continued, "could be considered *orlah*, fruit during its first three years of growth, which according to the Torah one may not harvest or consume." (Israel actually has detailed maps of Israeli orchards to monitor the trees so we can still observe this mitzvah today.)

The land of Israel is invested with sanctity and holiness. The Talmud (*Bava Batra* 158b) tells us that even the air in Israel is conducive to spiritual growth! And so, perhaps it's easier for people living in Israel to feel more spiritually connected, but what about those of us living outside of Israel – in New York, London, or Shanghai – where God's presence is not as readily felt? How are diaspora Jews expected to feel closer to God, especially during Elul, when that closeness is so important?

I think the answer can be found in the mitzvah of *bikkurim* – the mitzvah of the "first fruits" that we read about in *Parshat Ki Tavo* during the month of Elul. The Torah tells the farmer living in Israel that when he sees his first fruits of the season, before he can partake of any of his produce, he must first bring his fruit to Jerusalem and make the following declaration before the Kohen:

> My forefather was a wandering Aramean, and he went down to Egypt and sojourned there with a small number of people, and there, he became a great, mighty, and numerous nation. And the Egyptians treated us cruelly and afflicted us, and they imposed hard labor upon us. So we cried out to the Lord, God of our fathers, and the Lord heard our voice and saw our affliction, our toil, and our oppression. And the Lord brought us out from Egypt with a strong hand and with an outstretched arm, with great awe, and with signs and wonders. And He brought us to this place, and He gave us this land, a land flowing with milk and honey (Deuteronomy 26:5–9).

A farmer in biblical times couldn't just snatch a piece of fruit off the tree and eat it. He had to go through this whole ceremony and recite the long declaration before he could enjoy the rest of his harvest. Why? What's with all the pomp and circumstance over a little piece of fruit?

According to a contemporary rabbi – Rabbi Shalom Rosner, the *Bikkurim* ceremony impresses upon us the vital Jewish teaching that everything that happens to us in life, even a little fruit growing on a tree – is worthy of celebration and thanksgiving to God. The mitzvah of *bikkurim* teaches us that the little things in life are important.

Truthfully, there are really no "little" things. Everything that happens to us in this world is important because the world is governed by God. In the White House, for example, everything that happens is mapped out in advance. Nothing is left to chance because, after all, it's the White House. Similarly, everything in our world – because it's God's world – is orchestrated for a specific purpose and therefore even something "small" is worthy of ceremony and some pomp and circumstance.

That's why when the Jewish farmer sees his first fruit, he doesn't just pop one into his mouth. He brings it to Jerusalem and makes this whole declaration recalling the long road from slavery to freedom, from being an oppressed nation in Egypt to being self-sufficient in the land flowing with milk and honey. The farmer offers up his first fruits as an expression of gratitude to God.

Are we grateful for the little gifts that we sometimes take for granted in life? We may not live in Israel. We may not have the holiness of the land of Israel to inspire us this Elul. But we have food, we have clothing, and even here in New York we have some beautiful nature – limitless opportunities to express gratitude for the beautiful and small things in life. And so, before you pop some food into your mouth, try to first recite a blessing – expressing your gratitude since everything we are given to eat is a blessing. The food we eat in the diaspora may not have the holy status of *orlah*, and today we no longer perform the mitzvah of *bikkurim* (first fruits), but reciting blessings brings holiness into our everyday lives – wherever we live. If we're looking for something to feel more spiritually connected this Elul, reciting blessings before eating is an excellent way to go.

As Jews, we thank God for literally everything: For bread (after we wash our hands as the *kohanim* did before eating their tithed food), we say the blessing of *Baruch ata Ado-nay Eloheinu melech ha'olam ha-motzi lechem min ha-aretz,* "Blessed are You God who brings forth bread from the earth." For pastries and wheat products (using the first part as above), we say: *borei minei mezonot,* "God who creates various forms of sustenance." Even for a single grape or any other fruit, we say *borei pri ha-etz,* "God who creates the fruit of the tree." For vegetables we say *borei pri ha'adama,* "God who creates the fruit of the ground" and for everything else, we say *shehakol nihiyeh bidvaro,* "God who creates everything according to His word." These blessings are found in any Jewish prayer book, and they are a simple yet meaningful way to bring God and holiness into the world.

Yes, we work hard for what we have, but as Jews we must recognize and teach the world that success cannot come without God's blessing. The farmer in biblical times worked his land to see fruit, but the Torah instructed him to recognize God's providential role in bringing his ancestors out of Egypt, delivering them to a land of milk and honey and blessing him with fruit and produce. The material success we enjoy from our own hard work should never obscure God's role in the blessings we have. The mitzvah of *bikkurim* back in biblical times and the mitzvah of reciting blessings over food in our day teach us to be grateful for literally everything we have in our lives.

Question: What are three things for which you are truly grateful and which make you feel more connected to God? (They can even be the basics.)

_____

_____

_____

_____

Day 17
Bringing Redemption

ONE OF THE MOST CHALLENGING PARTS OF THE TORAH IS the *tochachah*, "the rebuke," when God informs the Jewish people of the dire consequences of failing to adhere to the Torah. The *tochachah* appears twice in the Torah, once in the book of Leviticus (chapter 26) and the second, in the book of Deuteronomy (chapter 28).

Both appearances of the *tochachah* remind us of the consequences of our actions, yet despite the parallels there is one noteworthy difference. The first admonition contains a silver lining in the verse which reads: "And I will remember My covenant with Jacob, and also My covenant with Isaac, and also My covenant with Abraham I will remember" (Leviticus 26:42). In this hopeful verse, God tells the Jewish people that no matter how bad things get, He will remember His people and ultimately intervene on our behalf. In the middle of this bleak picture, God provides us with a positive source of comfort and hope.

However, the rebuke in Deuteronomy does not have such a silver lining verse. It's hard to understand this deviation. Why does

God offer words of consolation in the first rebuke but not in the second?

The great medieval commentator Nachmanides explains that the two rebukes refer to the two different exiles that the Jewish people experienced. The first exile, at the hands of the Babylonians in 586 BCE, was relatively short, lasting only seventy years. After those seventy years had passed, God intervened to redeem the Jewish people, bringing our ancestors back to Israel. In fulfillment of the prophecy, God remembered the covenant and redeemed His people. However, the second exile, which took place at the hands of the Romans in 70 CE, was destined to be much longer. This is why, Nachmanides explains, the second rebuke contains no words of comfort. Because in regard to the second and longer exile – the one in which we continue to live – *we* will have to take an active part. God would redeem us from the first exile, but *we* must redeem ourselves from the second and current exile.

Rabbi Abraham Isaac Kook (1865–1935), the first Chief Rabbi of Israel, asked a simple question about a strange ritual we perform at the Passover Seder. Towards the end of the Seder, we get up from the table and open the door for the Prophet Elijah. Why, asks Rav Kook, do *we* need to get up and open the door? If Elijah can figure out how to stay alive all these centuries, and if he can find every Jewish home on the night of the Seder, surely Elijah can also figure out how to enter our homes! Maybe, he can pick the lock or squeeze through the keyhole. Why do we ourselves have to get up to let the Prophet Elijah in? Because the next *geulah* – the next redemption – says Rav Kook, will only come when the Jewish people get up and take action themselves.

Elijah represents redemption. Rav Kook is teaching that the next redemption is only going to come when the Jewish people take definitive action to spiritually improve our circumstances and redeem ourselves. Every time we perform a mitzvah, every time we study some Torah, every time we give charity or offer a comforting word – or visit Israel and support the Jewish State, encouraging people to return to Israel – we take one step closer to the redemption. Every time we engage in an act of kindness, pray, or support a Jewish cause we bring the ultimate redemption a little closer. And so, the second *tochachah* omits the words of consolation – that God will remember the covenant and redeem us – to teach us that *we* must bring the next redemption.

We perform mitzvot because we are commanded to do so and because they bring meaning and purpose to our personal lives. However, we also perform mitzvot to bring the world closer to redemption. Torah and mitzvot are not just for us. They are not just for the benefit of those performing them but for all humanity, to bring the entire world closer to its ultimate destination. Let us use this holy month of Elul to bring, not only ourselves closer to God, but the entire world closer to its final purpose – to the Messianic Redemption.

Question: Can you choose a mitzvah – one that you already do and one which you currently do not – which in your mind brings the world closer to God and to the Messianic redemption?

_____

_____

_____

_____

Day 18
Judging Favorably

ONE OF THE MOST IMPORTANT JEWISH PRINCIPLES IN interpersonal relations is the obligation to judge people favorably and to give others the benefit of the doubt (*Ethics of the Fathers* 1:6). This principle is relevant as we get closer to the High Holidays – to the "Days of Judgement" – because of the Jewish tradition that if we judge *others* favorably, God will judge *us* favorably (*Shabbat* 127b).

Rabbi Chaim Shmuelevitz, the great spiritual advisor of the Mir Yeshiva, asked an important question: Normally, the principle of judging favorably applies when there is incomplete information. We don't know if the person is acting appropriately or not, and the situation can be interpreted favorably or unfavorably. We don't know the underlying facts of the situation, only the surface-level appearance, and we don't have a full picture. In such cases, we are taught to fill in the missing pieces with a positive assumption. For example, if we know someone keeps kosher, but we observe them entering a McDonald's. In that situation, giving the person the benefit of the doubt would mean making the assumption that the person entered the restaurant for some reason other than to eat – perhaps to use the restrooms.

But how does this work with God? We are taught that if we give others the benefit of the doubt, God will do the same for us. But how can this be? After all, God is omniscient! He knows everything, so there's no data missing. If God knows everything – if He knows why the person went into McDonald's – what does it mean that He will judge us favorably? Doesn't God know if we acted properly or not?

Rabbi Shmuelevitz answers that in every human activity, there is some good and bad. Even when we do the right thing, there's usually *some* aspect that is done for personal gain. No action is a hundred percent motivated by pure altruism. Conversely, when we do something wrong, there is inevitably some good to those actions as well. The question is where we put our focus – on the positive or the negative? Since both good and bad exist within every action, we have a choice as to where we will direct our attention. Do we choose to see the good in people or the bad in people? Do we focus on the positive aspects of their character or areas where they fall short? Rabbi Shmuelevitz answers that whatever we choose to focus on in other people's lives, is what God will focus on in ours.

If we choose to direct our attention towards the good in others, even when we don't have the whole picture, God will focus on the good in us – even though He knows the whole situation. Conversely, if we focus on the bad in others, God will focus on that part of us as well. After all, how can we expect God to judge us more favorably than we judge others?

When we choose to actively overlook the negative aspects of other people's behavior, we're not being naive. It's making a choice to focus on the positive that also exists within our friend's conduct and character. Suppose a child wants to be helpful to his parents and starts cleaning the dishes, but because he is careless, a plate slips and shatters on the floor. The parent may naturally be upset with the child for not being careful, but they could instead choose to focus on how eager the child was to help out around the house. Both the child's desire to help and his carelessness are true. It becomes the parent's choice whether to focus on the positive or the negative, and it's a choice we all have to make as to where we should direct our attention.

The great Chasidic master, Rebbe Nachman of Breslov, wrote about the concept of judging others favorably as an overriding principle in Judaism. How do we look at other people? How do we look at life, and how do we even look at ourselves? If we get into the habit of routinely trying to find the good in others, over time we will train ourselves to always choose the good. Even when there's just a small chance that the motivation behind someone's questionable behavior is good, when we latch on to that good, we focus on the best in others and we become more positive people.

Still, judging others favorably can be challenging, especially when we feel wronged or offended in some way. One suggestion I have found helpful in judging others when feeling mistreated, is found in the very words of the Sages of the Mishnah: *havei dan et kol ha'adam l'kaf zechut*, "judge all people favorably" (*Ethics of the Fathers* 1:6). The Hebrew word *kol* or "all" would seem to suggest that we should judge "all" people favorably, and not just some people. However, there is another way to understand this phrase. The Hebrew term *kol ha'adam* can also be translated as "all of the person." We don't have to focus on the one wrong thing that person did and let that person be defined by that one action. We should not simply look at what the person did that offended us. Rather we can choose to look at *kol ha'adam*, at the whole person. Looking at the total person will not erase the wrong, but it will allow us to see the person's misdeed within the context of the entire person, including all their positive character traits and the good deeds they have performed. It helps us refrain from hyperfocusing on the one offense, and instead allows us to zoom the lens out and look at the entire person – a powerful technique to judge others favorably.

The more we choose to see the best in others, the more we will become the positive people we all want to be. Imagine what a different world it would be if we could latch on to whatever good we see in other people. And as our Sages teach, the more we do this for other people, the more God will do this for us.

Question: Reflect on a situation where you felt wronged by another person. Can you consider that there were circumstances in that person's life that could help you better understand why they behaved that way?

_____

_____

_____

_____

Day 19
Play the Ball, Not the Person

Before I say a word, I am its master. After I say a word, I am its slave.

– Rabbi Solomon ibn Gabirol, eleventh century

THIS PROFOUND STATEMENT, MADE BY THE MEDIEVAL POET and philosopher Rabbi Solomon ibn Gabirol, is truer today than ever before. In the age of the internet, when so many people are listening and watching everything we say, we need to remember that once we say something, it's out there and sometimes hard to take back.

There is a famous story about an individual who loved to gossip about other people in his small community. He didn't care if the rumors were true, or who they hurt. He just loved to share the latest, juiciest gossip about other people. One day, he realized that Rosh Hashanah was around the corner, and he was overtaken by contrition. He went to the local rabbi and asked, "Rabbi, how can I make good on all the wrong I've done?

"There is one thing you can do," said the rabbi, "but you must do exactly as I say." The man promised, clearly driven by the desire to make things right.

"Do you have a pillow at home?" asked the rabbi, and the man nodded yes. "Go home, rip open a pillow, empty out the feathers, and place one feather in front of the home of each person you slandered. When you're done, come back to me for the second set of instructions."

The next day, the man returned. "Rabbi, I did exactly what you said. Now what?"

"Now," the rabbi replied, "go back to each person's house, collect the feathers, and bring them to me."

"Rabbi, that's impossible," the man cried, "they've all blown away!"

The rabbi of course was teaching his congregant an important lesson. Once something is out there, we can't simply take it back.

One of the main prayers of Yom Kippur is the *Al Chet* confessional, an alphabetical listing of our sins. Many of the sins we acknowledge and for which we seek forgiveness have to do with speech – how we express ourselves and what we say about other people. Whether we have used improper language, spoken falsely, pressured someone to do something they didn't want to do, given a false confession, or just spoken foolishly. Today because of the internet – because we have so much more access to other people – our speech has even more impact than ever before.

Before the internet, it was challenging to get a large following. Unless you were a famous reporter or TV personality, most people would not really know of your existence. Today, all you need to do is post something on social media, and within a few seconds, it can be seen by hundreds of people and, if it goes viral, thousands, even millions.

Now, that doesn't mean that we shouldn't speak up and express what we feel on important issues. Every Friday night as part of the *Kabbalat Shabbat* service ("Welcoming the Sabbath"), we recite the verse, "Those who love God should despise evil" (Psalm 97:10). If you hear someone say something you feel is wrong or immoral, it is appropriate to say something but, as they say in basketball, "Play the ball, not the man" – tackle the issue, not the person expressing the point of view.

Too often, we personalize the argument. We get caught up in *who* shared the idea rather than the relative strengths and weaknesses of the idea itself. We've gotten too used to attacking the person with whom we disagree, instead of the argument they are making. We see this amongst our politicians, journalists, social media outlets, and sometimes in ourselves.

Within Jewish tradition, we have what's called a *machloket l'shaim shmayim* – a "dispute for the sake of Heaven." The great Sages of the Talmud debated fundamental issues of thought and practice but never made their arguments personal. These were highly educated and thoughtful individuals who respected each other but still legitimately disagreed on important issues. As our Talmudic tradition of argument and debate bears out, a clash of views is how truth emerges. The English philosopher John Stuart Mill famously wrote, "it is only by the collision of adverse opinions, that the remainder of the truth has any chance of being supplied."

But this kind of exchange can only happen when there is respect. The Sages of the Talmud had that respect for one another, even as they vehemently disagreed on core questions of faith and law. The best example of this were the two great intellectual adversaries of the Talmud, Hillel and Shammai. When these two great scholars argued, their positions were always expressed as coming from the "House of Hillel" and "House of Shammai," because as people Hillel and Shamai greatly respected one another. The Mishnah (oral tradition) records that despite their disagreements regarding marriage and divorce, they did not prevent their respective followers and students from marrying one another.

We seem to have lost that ability of remaining pleasant and agreeable when we are confronted with an idea we do not like. This does not mean we need to agree with every position out there, nor does it mean we must keep quiet when hearing something we think offensive or wrong in some way. What it does mean is to refrain from personalizing the issue by shifting the focus from the individual back to the idea.

If we really are arguing for "the sake of Heaven" we will discuss the issue – not the people making the arguments – because that will ultimately enable us to arrive at the best resolution. Attacking the other person may make us feel better and allow us to "score points," but in the end it is counterproductive. Perhaps this is what the Mishnah means when it teaches: "Any dispute for the sake of Heaven will endure and any dispute that is not for the sake of Heaven will not endure" (*Ethics of the Fathers* 5:17). If we are sincere about our position, and we therefore focus on the substance of the issue and not the people, something positive will come out of it.

As we prepare for the days of awe, we will do well to remember the wise words of Rabbi Solomon ibn Gabirol: "Before I say a word, I am its master. After I say a word, I am its slave."

Question: How can you maintain polite and respectful dialogue with someone you disagree with? What methods would you employ to debate the merits of an idea, rather than the character of the person themselves?

_____

_____

_____

_____

Day 20
Halfway There! Looking Ahead

ON THE FIRST DAY OF OUR FORTY-DAY CHALLENGE, WHEN we began our journey, we spoke about the significance of Rosh Chodesh Elul – the first day of the Hebrew month of Elul. We studied how that was the day Moshe was called back up to Mount Sinai – to give the Jewish people a second chance and a second set of tablets. If you remember, when Moshe first came down from Mount Sinai and saw the Jews sinning with the Golden Calf, he broke the tablets (the first set) and then prayed on behalf of the Jewish people for forty days. On Rosh Chodesh Elul, God invited Moshe back to Mount Sinai for the second set of tablets, giving the Jews another chance. Moshe reascended the mountain on Rosh Chodesh Elul and spent another forty days and nights with God, coming back down on Yom Kippur.

The number forty is therefore quite significant. It's the number of days which lapsed between the first time Moshe brought down the tablets and when he was invited back up for the second set, and it is also the amount of time between Rosh Chodesh Elul and Yom Kippur – when the Torah was re-given to Moshe.

Consider all the other instances of forty in Jewish tradition: forty is the number of days the flood ravaged and transformed the world in the days of Noah; forty is the amount of *se'ot* (a liquid measure of water) which is required for a *mikvah*, a Jewish ritual bath which is a source of spiritual renewal and transformation. A fetus is considered to be endowed with a soul – and not merely tissue – after forty days. Our ancestors wandered in the wilderness for forty years. Rabbi Akiva – arguably the greatest sage of the Talmud, returned to Judaism at the age of forty. And according to the Talmud (*Avodah Zarah* 5b), a student does not fully comprehend his teacher's Torah until he has studied under him for forty years.

The number forty represents metamorphosis and transformation. In *gematria* (Hebrew alpha-numeric correspondence), the number forty is represented by the letter *mem*, which is the first letter of the word *mayim*, meaning "water." Water transforms, cleanses, and purifies, and that is precisely what we are going through these forty days from Rosh Chodesh Elul to Yom Kippur – a process of purification, growth, and rebirth.

But real change takes time. Transformation does not happen overnight and so the number representing change is forty – not one or two, because time is needed to see significant growth. And the goal is not to radically change ourselves into someone totally different – that is simply unrealistic – but instead, to focus on one or two aspects of our personality and character that could use some refining.

I recently received an email which upset me. I was about to fire back a quick and angry response, but I remembered what I shared on Day 6 of our Forty-Day Challenge: take a moment, breathe, and don't respond in anger. I recalled Abraham Lincoln's "hot letters" – the letters he would write to cool down. At the bottom of these hot letters, he still had the presence of mind to write, "Never Signed, Never Sent." That extra level of consciousness, which I personally developed just from writing that entry, made a difference. When we resolve to make small but mindful improvements in our lives, real change is possible.

We've hit the halfway mark, having studied together now for the last twenty days. As we look ahead to the next twenty, ask yourself: in what area of life would you like to see some change? Whether it's working on your interpersonal relationships, Shabbat observance, or reciting blessings before eating, my suggestion is to choose one mitzvah in the realm of your relationship with God (*kashrut*, prayer, *tefillin*, etc.) and one mitzvah in regard to your fellow human beings (charity, acts of kindness, visiting the sick, positive speech, etc.). Also, think about one character flaw in your personality and how you think you can make a change. As we learned on Day 2, we can only achieve positive change if we're honest with ourselves about areas of improvement. Then visualize where you would like to be in twenty days – by the time Yom Kippur arrives. Imagine yourself observing that new mitzvah and how that character flaw can be improved.

Twenty days is a good amount of time to see some change. Even if it's small, it will be real, helping to cleanse and elevate ourselves just in time for Yom Kippur, the ultimate day of transformation and purification.

Question: Looking back at the past entries, what new insight about yourself, other people, Judaism, or God have you discovered?

_____

_____

_____

_____

Day 21
Selichot

THE 1996 MOTION PICTURE *JERRY MAGUIRE* WAS ABOUT A sports agent who developed a conscience and a sense of mission. Jerry – portrayed by Tom Cruise – tries to win back his co-worker and future girlfriend Dorothy, played by Renée Zellweger. Jerry arrives at Dorothy's home and delivers a stirring monologue including the famous words, "You complete me." Dorothy then responds to Jerry with the immortal words, "You had me at 'hello.'"

There are words that can reset relationships. These positive triggers have the power to remind people of the true love they share.

Our relationship with God is no different. There are some special words Jews recite each year as a way of rekindling our relationship with God during the High Holiday season. Those words form the *Selichot*, the special penitential prayers we begin reciting before Rosh Hashanah. (Sephardic Jews recite *Selichot* for the entire month of Elul, whereas the Ashkenazi practice is to begin them on the Saturday night before Rosh Hashanah.)

The source for reciting *Selichot* is a tenth-century rabbinic text called the *Tanna De-Vei Eliyahu*, which records a vision King David had of a conversation between himself and God (Hashem). In this conversation, David asks God how his descendants, the Jewish people, would earn forgiveness for their sins once the Temple is destroyed. King David understood that it was through the Temple service that Jews obtained atonement for the wrongs they had committed throughout the year, but through his prophetic vision, King David learned that the Temple would one day be destroyed, and the Jewish people would be left without this means of atonement. In distress, David asks God, "How will the Jewish people earn forgiveness and reconnect to You once the Temple is in ruins?"

In response, David received a vision of God Himself wrapped in a *tallit* (a prayer shawl), like a cantor leading services, showing Moshe the special "Thirteen Attributes of Mercy," which make up the central part of the *Selichot* service: "Hashem, Hashem, God, Compassionate, and Gracious, Slow to anger, and Abundant in Kindness and Truth, Preserver of Kindness for thousands of generations, Forgiver of iniquity, willful sin, and error, and Who cleanses" (Exodus 34:6–7).

These words reflect the special attributes of the Divine, focusing on God's compassion and mercy. God Himself taught these words to Moshe in the immediate aftermath of the sin of the Golden Calf. After the Jews had sinned, God told Moshe to teach the people to use this special prayer whenever the people would need to obtain God's forgiveness. The *Selichot* are thus God's way of giving us a spiritual way back to Himself, after we have distanced ourselves through sin.

Ultimately, God was telling David that even after the Temple would be destroyed, there would always be a way for the Jewish people to find their way back. When other avenues of spiritual connection are closed off, the special Thirteen Attributes of Mercy – the *Selichot* prayers – are always there for us to use to reconcile. That is why we repeatedly recite the Thirteen Attributes at the

Ne'ilah service – at the apex of the Yom Kippur service – when we beseech God and get in our last requests before the gates of prayer are closed.

It's like a parent saying to their child, "Inevitably you will make mistakes in life, but here is what you can do when you want to rectify the damage: apologize and admit your wrongdoing, express remorse and resolve to do better in the future, and make sure we stay connected by using these words."

"To err is human, to forgive is divine." God knows sin is inevitable and that those sins will create distance. To ensure that distance does not last too long, in His infinite mercy and love, God gives us the words of the *Selichot* as a way to restore the relationship. The *Selichot* and the Thirteen Attributes of Mercy are ultimately an expression of God's interest in maintaining an intimate relationship with His creations.

That is the way to ensure we stay close with God – and with our fellow man, which is why we also have the tradition between Rosh Hashanah and Yom Kippur to ask people we've wronged to forgive us. It's our time to repair *all* our relationships – with people and with God – that have sustained some damage over the past year.

Think about King David's vision of a caring God, in the aftermath of the sin of the Golden Calf, teaching His faithful servant Moshe this special prayer. Think of Hashem telling David that even when the Temple is in ruins – and when we feel like there is no tangible way to reconnect – there is always a way back. Take advantage of the Thirteen Attributes. Ideally, they should be recited in Hebrew in synagogue with a *minyan*. If you are unable to, then recite them on your own in English. They are God's gift to us for us to use at this special time.

As the prophet Isaiah declared, "Seek out God while He may be found, call upon Him while He is near" (55:6).

Thirteen Attributes of Mercy – Translated and Explained

1. HASHEM – HASHEM is merciful before man sins.
2. HASHEM – HASHEM is merciful after the sin.
3. Kel (God) – the power of Hashem's mercy.
4. Rachum (Compassionate) – Hashem eases the punishment of those being punished.
5. Chanun (Gracious) – God is gracious even to those who don't deserve it.
6. Erech Apayim (Slow to anger) – God gives time for the sinner to repent.
7. v'Rav Chesed (and Abundant in Kindness) – God shows *chesed* to those without personal merits. God removes sins from the scales, to give more merit.
8. v'Emes (and Truth) – God's promise to forgive is irrevocable.
9. Notzer chesed l'alafim (Preserver of kindness for thousands of generations) – those who perform mitzvot benefit their offspring.
10. Nosei avon (Forgiver of iniquity) – God will even forgive those who sin intentionally, if they do *teshuvah* (repentance).
11. Va'Fesha (Forgiver of willful sin) – God will even forgive those who sin intentionally with the purpose of rebelling.
12. v'Chataah (Forgiver of error) – why are lesser iniquities mentioned after the more severe ones? Because God's mercy can transform intentional error to small errors; we then ask for forgiveness for the small ones.
13. v'Nakeh (and who cleanses) – God wipes away the sins of those who repent seriously.*

---

* We have followed Rabbeinu Tam's opinion of the Thirteen Attributes (*Rosh Hashanah* 17b), as explained by the ArtScroll *siddur*.

By thinking about what these attributes mean, and how we relate to God in so many different ways, we can make the relationship stronger than ever before.

Question: How can you emulate God's trait of compassion in dealing with any of your colleagues at work or family members at home?

_____

_____

_____

_____

Day 22
Not in Heaven

THE GREAT RAMBAM PENNED A LETTER TO A SIMPLE JEW IN Baghdad named Joseph Ibn Gabir. Joseph, not knowing any Hebrew, was unable to read the *Mishneh Torah*, the Rambam's major work on Jewish Law. Gabir therefore asked the Rambam to respond in his own hand and to give him some encouragement.

In response, Rambam wrote: "First of all, I must tell you, may the Lord keep and increase your welfare, that you are not justified in regarding yourself as an *am ha-aretz* (ignoramus). You are our beloved pupil; so is everybody who is desirous of studying even one verse or a single law. It also makes no difference whether you study in the holy language [Hebrew], or in Arabic [the vernacular], or in Aramaic [the language of the Talmud]; it matters only whether it is done with understanding... But of the man who neglects the development of his spirit it is said 'He has despised the word of the Lord' (Num. 15:31); this applies also to a man who fails to continue his studies even if he has become a great scholar, for the advancement of learning is the highest command. I say, therefore, in general, that you must not belittle yourself nor give up the intention of improving. There are great scholars who did not begin their studies until an advanced age, and who became scholars of distinction in spite of this" (Isadore Twersky, *A Maimonides Reader*, p. 478).

Judaism is supposed to be attainable. Although at times we might be intimidated by the intricacies and complexity of the Torah's many laws, commentaries, and philosophical treatises, it is supposed to be something within our reach. As the Torah itself declares: "It is not in Heaven, that you should say, 'Who will ascend into Heaven for us and bring it to us, that we may hear it and do it?' Nor is it beyond the sea, that you should say, 'Who will go over the sea for us and bring it to us, that we may hear it and do it?' Rather the matter is very near you, in your mouth and in your heart, that you may do it" (Deuteronomy 30:12–14).

Judaism is not esoteric or unreachable. It's not in the heavens. Even if it feels like Torah is a world away or on the other side of the planet – that may be the way we feel – but it's not the true reality. As the verse teaches, the Torah is "very near you, in your mouth and in your heart."

But why does the last verse quoted above read "in your mouth and in your heart"? After all, our mouths should ideally reflect what's in our hearts, not vice versa. And so, shouldn't the order be reversed – shouldn't the Torah have instead said: in your heart and in your mouth? Why is the mouth mentioned before the heart?

The following story can help answer the question. Rabbi Aryeh Levin, known as the tzaddik of Jerusalem, was famous for visiting imprisoned Jews during the British Mandate. The rabbi would visit the Jewish soldiers who were incarcerated by the British for fighting for Jewish independence before the modern State of Israel was established. Rabbi Levin was allowed by the British to visit these Jewish inmates, and he set up a makeshift synagogue inside the prison so they could pray together on Shabbat.

One Shabbat, one of the more cynical prisoners approached

Rabbi Levin and objected, "Don't you realize that these people are fakes? They all put on a *yarmulke* a minute before you arrive, and as soon as you leave, they take out their cigarettes and start to smoke (which is forbidden on Shabbat). Why do you waste your time with these liars?"

"I'm a very short man," Rabbi Levin responded, "so I can't see the top of their heads to see if they're wearing a *yarmulke* or not. All I can see is their hearts."

We don't really know what's going on in the hearts of other people. Sometimes we don't even understand what's happening in our own hearts. Nor can we always control what happens within, but we can control what we say and how we use our words. Therefore, the Torah says "mouth" before it says "heart" because speech is within our power. We can control how we use our words when speaking with our friends, co-workers, and loved ones. We can control how often we pray to God. The Jewish inmates may certainly have been inconsistent by praying with Rabbi Levin and then later smoking on Shabbat. However, they still took the time to pray, to cover their heads with a *yarmulke*, and to recite words of prayer to the Almighty.

When the Torah tells us that Judaism is near to us "in your mouth and in your heart," it's telling us to first make sure we say the right thing. Make sure to pray to Hashem even when you are not feeling motivated internally, because how we articulate ourselves to God in prayer and what we say to our fellow human beings is what ultimately impacts the way we feel in our heart. The Torah puts the mouth before the heart, because we can influence the heart with our mouths and with our words – by what we say and how we pray. While we cannot always control what we feel internally, we can control our behavior. As we've quoted the well-known adage of the *Sefer Ha-Chinuch*: "after one's actions follows one's heart."

As we get closer to the High Holidays, let's focus on saying and doing the right thing, both to our colleagues and friends, and in our praying to Hashem. Doing so will not only impact us internally, but it will ensure that the Torah remains, not in the heavens or beyond the sea, but within our heart.

Question: Name one area of Jewish observance which seems remote or foreign to you. What is one step you can take to bring yourself closer to that area of Jewish tradition?

_____

_____

_____

_____

Day 23
The Stork

IN OUR FIRST ENTRY, WE MENTIONED THAT THE HEBREW month Elul is made up of the letters *alef, lamed, vav, lamed,* and that these letters spell out two different messages. In relation to God, the letters spell out the biblical verse – *ani l'dodi v'dodi li,* "I am for my beloved and my beloved is mine" (Song of Songs 6:3); and in regard to our fellow human beings, they spell out the verse – *ish l'reyeihu u'matanot l'evyonim,* "one person for his friend and gifts to the poor" (Esther 9:22). This represents another way of spiritually reconnecting during the month of Elul – by helping the less fortunate and being there for our friends.

This second verse, taken from the Scroll of Esther (Megillah), is the biblical source for the Jewish tradition to give charity to the poor – specifically on Purim – as a way to celebrate the miracle of Purim, namely, the saving of Persian Jewry from Haman's evil decree. But who is thinking about Purim at this time on the Jewish calendar? Purim is celebrated in either February or March of each year and now we are in September or October, so why are we referencing the holiday of Purim now?

Because the mitzvah of *tzedakah,* or charity, is not limited to

Purim or any one time of the year; sharing our blessings with those less fortunate is a mitzvah to be performed all year round. We must always be developing our sense of compassion and caring towards those around us. And so, giving charity must be something we do at all times, and in every part of the year.

Interestingly, this idea of sharing our bounty with others is expressed by a specific type of bird – the *chasidah* or the stork, which the Torah tells us is not kosher, and therefore is forbidden to be eaten. (Leviticus 11:19, Deuteronomy 14:18). The great biblical commentator Rashi raises the question: why is the stork called a *chasidah*, which derives from the Hebrew word *chesed*, meaning "kindness"? Rashi, quoting the Talmud (*Chullin* 63a) answers: "Because it deals kindly with its friends in respect to food" (Rashi on Leviticus 11:19).

But why is the stork not considered a kosher bird if it acts in such a praiseworthy manner? Rambam, one of the great Jewish philosophers, wrote that the birds which the Torah lists as non-kosher are listed as such because they display acts of cruelty. Other sages also suggest this idea behind the Torah prohibiting certain animals, namely, to prevent us from adopting and internalizing the cruel tendencies of these forbidden animals. Then why is the stork – which literally draws its very name from the kindness it does with its friends – not considered kosher?

The commentaries answer this question by asking another question: to whom does the stork extend her *chesed* (kindness)? Rashi says that the stork is generous to its friends. My mentor Rabbi Dr. Jacob J. Schachter explains that any living thing which expresses kindness only with its friends is unfit for Jewish consumption. Elul is a time of *ish l'reyeihu u'matanot l'evyonim*, "one person for his friend and gifts to the poor." Our obligation extends to all people, not just to our friends. This is something we need to think about during this time of year. What are we doing to help those who we do not know? To those who maybe don't look like us, dress like us, or have the same backgrounds that we do? What are we doing to alleviate other people's distress?

There's an old adage that charity begins at home and this indeed is a Jewish teaching. As the Talmud famously teaches: "the poor of one's own city come first" (*Bava Metzia* 71a). We are expected to sustain those closest to us first, so if there's somebody within our smaller orbit of life – a relative, a friend or colleague who needs help – then our responsibility goes to helping them first.

At the same time, while charity begins at home, charity does not end at home. We are supposed to look beyond our own circle and help others on the outside. The *chasidah*, the stork, takes care of her friends in her inner orbit, but falls short of showing generosity to those outside her circle.

This must be an important part of our Forty-Day Challenge: How will we, during this month of Elul – as we prepare for the High Holidays – go out of our comfort zone to help people outside of our own circle? Again, if there is someone in great need in our family or inner circle, we must begin by helping them. But once our family and friends are taken care of, we must venture out further into the community and extend a helping hand to those on the outside.

There are many ways to do this. Here are three simple suggestions:

1. Donate money to those in need. There are many excellent organizations that collect for the Jewish poor, both in the United States and in Israel, as well as not-for-profits which raise money for other vital causes.

2. Find a soup kitchen where you can serve food to poor people who don't have the means to purchase meals for themselves. In New York, Masbia is a wonderful Jewish (and kosher) establishment

in Brooklyn, New York, where you can go to prepare meals for the poor. I went with my family to peel potatoes and chop onions and you can serve the food as well.

3. Participate in the great mitzvah of *bikkur cholim* by visiting the sick and elderly in hospitals and nursing homes. Our neighborhoods abound with hospitals and nursing homes filled with countless people who are alone and in need of greater human contact.

Engaging in any one of these acts of kindness (*chesed*) will not only put a smile on someone else's face, it will fill you with meaning and warmth like nothing else can. On Sunday outings, our family always gets so much more out of doing *chesed* projects (delivering food packages to the poor) than when we do something "for the kids." We always come back feeling closer to each other and with a shared sense of fulfillment from helping others.

Elul is our time to draw closer to God and to our fellow human beings. Giving charity and performing acts of kindness are indispensable ways of achieving that closeness.

Question: Choose one act of kindness you can perform by Yom Kippur for someone, or for some group, outside of your inner circle.

_____

_____

_____

_____

Day 24
Silence

A fence for wisdom is silence.
– *Pirkei Avot* 3:13

CALVIN COOLIDGE, THE THIRTIETH PRESIDENT OF THE United States, was known for not being a big talker. His taciturnity was so famous that one evening, at a dinner party, a woman approached "Silent Cal" and said, "Mr. President, I have made a bet for a large sum of money that I would be able to get you to say at least three words."

The President turned to the lady and slowly responded, "You lose."

We're always looking for the right words. We constantly ask ourselves: "What should I say?" "How should I respond?" The great Rambam wrote that a person should not be quick to respond or speak just for the sake of speaking. He cautioned teachers against gratuitously adding on words when teaching but instead recommended speaking simply and pleasantly without raising one's voice, quoting the rabbinic adage: "the words of the Sages are heard pleasantly." Saying more isn't always better.

The idea of not always having to say something is an important

Jewish value. We often feel compelled to have something to say in every situation, or we feel pressured to say "the right thing." I used to feel this pressure when paying my respects at a *shiva* call, the seven days of mourning following the passing of a close relative. I will never forget an experience I had when I myself was sitting *shiva*, following the passing of my mother, of blessed memory. At one point during the *shiva*, among the many visitors were a number of rabbis, about six or seven who showed at the same time and for some reason, I just didn't feel like talking. The rabbis present were well aware of the Jewish tradition not to initiate conversation at a *shiva* home, but rather to leave it to the mourner to speak or not to speak. Since I didn't say anything, they didn't say anything either. All the other visitors took their cues from the rabbis and so, there we were, about thirty people sitting in a room completely quiet. The silence was powerful. I felt the entire room's warm embrace, and no one hugged me or said a word. Just silence.

It's twenty-five years since that experience, and what I remember bringing me comfort and solace from the whole *shiva* experience were those few minutes of quiet. I remember thinking at the time that there are no words anyone could share to make me feel better about my mother's passing, but just sitting with my friends, colleagues, and teachers made a real difference. It was their presence which brought me comfort, not their words. I try to remember this every time I go and pay a *shiva* call, and I share this story with those who are nervous about what to say in a *shiva* home. What brings comfort to others is not some kitschy phrase, clever line, or theological explanation, but simply being there.

Silence is also an important Jewish virtue because it makes it easier to hear other people. When we're always looking for the right words to say ourselves, there's not much room left to hear what the people around us are saying. When we can truly hear others, we can align ourselves to *their* needs and not just our own. And then when we do choose to speak, we are more likely to say things that are useful to other people, not just to ourselves.

Modern society idealizes the witty response and sarcastic repartee. And this is only exacerbated on social media, which is driven by the idea that we need to have a "comment" for everything. We're encouraged to tell the world what we "like" or "love," and we're constantly prompted to fill the internet with our words and emojis. But where do those comments really get us? Do they present the best version of ourselves? Are those comments reflecting who we truly are or compassion for the people around us? Social media posts conveying important information or insightful thoughts can be a wonderful way of educating and promoting good values, but gratuitous comments – simply designed to get us more "likes" – cheapen us and diminish the power of our words.

The great sage Rabbi Yehuda Ha-Nasi shared that one of his students, simply known as "Rav" never spoke an unnecessary word in his entire life. Rambam goes so far as to hold this out as an ideal ("Laws of Character Traits" 2:8). This may seem a bit extreme, but it teaches us that even when it is appropriate for us to speak, it's a good idea to be measured and temperate with our words. If all we do is talk, there's not enough room left to listen, learn, or love. In a world filled with idle chatter, transient prattle, and empty words, the value of silence begins to emerge.

We don't need to go to Rav's extreme. To foster meaningful relationships and share important information we must be able to speak freely, but it's important to remember that our words represent who we are and how we are perceived. Our words can indicate that we are attuned to the people around us or demonstrate that we are focused only on ourselves. And sometimes, like at a *shiva*, the best words are no words at all.

Question: In general, when you speak with others do you aim to listen and genuinely hear them out? Think of one or two situations in which being more silent can help you be more receptive to what is being said.

_____

_____

_____

_____

Day 25
Focus Amidst the Static

WHAT REMINDS YOU OF YOUR PURPOSE AND MISSION IN life?

After high school, during my gap year abroad studying in Israel, I had the privilege of studying under the great Rabbi Avigdor Nebenzahl, then the Chief Rabbi of the Old City of Jerusalem. Rabbi Nebenzahl, may he live and be well, is an extremely erudite and scholarly individual, but also exceedingly humble and he was uncomfortable with people taking pictures of him. He didn't want people putting him on a pedestal. However, one of my other teachers asked Rav Nebenzahl if we could take a picture of him before we went back to America.

"These boys," he explained to Rav Nebenzahl, "are going off to college. They will have a lot of distractions and temptations in the next few years. A picture of you in their dorm room can be of great help in reminding them of their purpose." The rabbi graciously agreed. To this day, my picture of Rav Nebenzahl – and some of my other teachers – still hang on my dining room wall, continuing to influence and inspire me and my family.

What keeps you inspired as to your purpose and mission in life?

How do you stay focused on your priorities in a world so filled with distractions?

Although all Jews are commanded to write a Torah scroll, or to have one written for them, a Jewish king is obligated to write two scrolls – one which he would keep in the palace, and one he took with him wherever he went. In fact, according to one opinion in the Talmud, the Jewish king had that Torah scroll hanging from his very arm (*Sanhedrin* 22a). The symbolism of a king carrying a Torah scroll wherever he traveled is very powerful. Even though the king was mighty, and enjoyed privileges of rulership, he was still answerable to a higher authority. The king, despite his grandeur and fame, was still obligated to remain connected to his spiritual source. The additional Torah scroll – ever-present and following him wherever he went – served as a sort of checks-and-balances for the king so he would never forget his mission of bringing Godliness to the world.

What "Torah scroll" do we carry around with us? What reminders do we have in our lives that keep us connected to our ultimate purpose and mission? There are challenges and distractions all around us, and Judaism can also sometimes feel esoteric and unattainable (we have discussed the fact that Judaism is always attainable in Day 22, "Not in Heaven"). Still, the God in which we believe cannot be seen or experienced with any of our physical senses, so what can we do that feels concrete and tangible to keep us focused on our mission in life?

The Torah has a number of commandments that serve as reminders for our purpose in life. We hang a *mezuzah* – a hand-written parchment containing the *Shema* sealed in a small case – on the doorposts in our homes. The *mezuzah* reminds us that whether we're coming or going, we have a purpose both at home and out in the world.

Men are commanded to wear *tzitzit*, to attach strings to a four-cornered fringed garment, "so that you may look upon it and remember all the commandments of God and perform them, and not wander after your heart and your eyes that lead you astray" (Numbers 15:39). The Torah acknowledges that life is full of distractions and challenges to our faith, and the *tzitzit* remind us of our higher purpose.

The Torah also tells us the tassels on the *tzitzit* should have a thread of blue, called *techeilet* (Ibid. 15:38). The Talmud says this azure blue must come from the *chilazon*, a type of aquatic creature or snail whose identity was forgotten long ago, and for centuries Jews were unable to properly fulfill this mitzvah of *techeilet*. However, the identity of the *chilazon* has recently been rediscovered, and we are witnessing a renaissance in this mitzvah of *techeilet*.

But why should we make such a fuss about finding this obscure blue dye? Because it too serves as a reminder. According to the Talmud, that blue thread dangling from our *tzitzit* reminds us of the ocean, and the ocean reminds us of the sky, and the sky reminds us of the Heavenly Throne, i.e., God Himself (*Menachot* 23b).

The *tefillin* also serve this purpose. Each morning, men literally wrap boxes containing parchments with verses from the Torah on their arms and heads. One should of course always be thinking about the ideas contained in those verses, but it's easier when they are wrapped around your arm and head. The *tefillin* worn on the arm are also angled inward, towards the heart. When we wear the head *tefillin* and hand *tefillin* together, we are demonstrating our desire to unify our mind, heart, and actions. Similarly, we should always think of God, but wearing a *yarmulke* (*kippah*) on our heads helps us remain mindful of God above us.

Even though God is incorporeal and totally spiritual, we are not. Physical beings need physical reminders. We require tangible signs of our purpose and mission. As the great scholar Rabbi Samson Raphael Hirsch (nineteenth century) notes, some commandments are called *edot* – or "testimonies" – because they literally testify to our purpose in life.

We do not worship that which is physical, nor should any of these religious objects become the point of our devotion. Instead, the *mezuzot, tzitzit,* and *tefillin* are used to keep us aware of our mission and to channel our focus to our spiritual source. This is also why we pray three times a day, using the same words for each prayer service. Because we are so easily distracted from pursuing our spiritual goals, we need words and other physical reminders that will inspire us to stay focused.

What reminders do we have in our home or on ourselves? Do we have candlesticks for Shabbat, a *mezuzah* on our doorposts, and Jewish books on our shelves? Do we wear *tzitzit* and *tefillin* – even if only for short periods of time during the day – to serve as reminders of our mission and purpose? The prayers may seem repetitive, but the Sages understood our need for continual reminders.

We're not robots who can simply be programmed and then run on our own. "Set it and forget it" doesn't work when it comes to our spiritual development. We get caught up in the everyday distractions of life and sometimes forget what is most important or we just need some inspiration to keep us going. That reminder or inspiration cannot always come from within, so we turn to external surroundings – a *mezuzah,* Shabbat candles, *tzitzit, tefillin,* or a prayer book. These "reminders" are all prescribed by the Torah and so they carry greater weight but the right background image on your laptop or cellphone could also be a great reminder. It could be a photograph of someone who inspires you, like a mentor, teacher, or a grandparent.

Do we have enough physical reminders or objects of inspiration in our homes? At a time such as now, when we are trying to become the very best version of ourselves, these reminders can go a long way.

Question: What physical object(s) do you currently possess or can you consider obtaining that can be used as a source of inspiration for greater spirituality and which can help motivate you to stay more focused amidst the many distractions in your life?

_____

_____

_____

_____

Day 26
The Purpose of Rosh Hashanah

VIRTUALLY EVERY YEAR, I RECEIVE THE SAME QUESTION from my students: "Rabbi, if one of the purposes of Rosh Hashanah is to obtain forgiveness for our sins, then why don't the Rosh Hashanah prayers mention anything about forgiveness?"

It's a good question, because when you take a look at the *machzor* – the Rosh Hashanah prayer book – the idea of forgiveness is virtually absent from the liturgy. There are a few mentions of the "Day of Judgement" and the idea that we are being evaluated by God, but the liturgy revolves around basic Jewish concepts such as our belief in a One God who is King and Sovereign of the Universe. The pleading and begging for forgiveness – which seem so critical to the High Holidays – seem to be left for the *Selichot* (which we discussed on Day 21) and for Yom Kippur, but not for Rosh Hashanah.

Why do Rosh Hashanah prayers omit the theme of forgiveness?

Our relationship with God – as with any being – needs to follow a logical progression. Before we can ask God for forgiveness, we need to first ask ourselves a few basic questions: Who is God? Who are we? And who are we in *relation* to God? It makes little sense to plead for forgiveness before we understand our relationship with God. That is precisely why the three central themes of the Rosh Hashanah prayers are *Malchiyot* (Kingship), *Zichronot* (Remembrances), and *Shofarot* (Trumpet Blasts). These themes – not atonement or forgiveness – make up the *Amidah* (Silent Devotion), the main prayer in the *Musaf* service of Rosh Hashanah.

The theme of *Malchiyot* (Kingship) is paramount on Rosh Hashanah. It is the first theme of the *Musaf* prayer service and it sets up the nature of our relationship with God. In the *Malchiyot* section, we acknowledge that God is King over the universe and that we are His loyal subjects. The only reason we feel compelled to ask forgiveness from God is that we feel obligated as subjects to adhere to the King's wishes.

The middle theme is *Zichronot*, which means "Remembrances." This section refers to our belief in a God who remembers everything. Although the idea that God remembers all we have done can be daunting, it also demonstrates how much God cares about us. When a parent disciplines a child, that shows a relationship is present. Critique or judgment, if done with love, demonstrate that the parent wants what's best for the child. It's far worse if the parent simply ignores their child than for a parent to bring up a past misdeed of their son or daughter, because that shows there is no relationship to be salvaged. When a parent disciplines a child and provides constructive criticism, the parent shows their love and affection. A child neglected is a child unloved.

The final theme of the Rosh Hashanah prayers is *Shofarot* or "Trumpet Blasts," which recalls the *shofar* sounded at the giving of the Torah at Sinai. This represents the idea that God is not only a sovereign King but a Being who provides us with a spiritual path to live in the world. A mortal king can be aloof and indifferent to the welfare of his subjects. The *Shofarot* section teaches that God wants to be intimately involved in our lives. He therefore provides us with the Torah, which operates as a guidebook so we can go through life in the best possible way, helping us achieve the very purpose for creation.

Our goal on Rosh Hashanah is therefore to establish the true nature of our relationship with God. It is a relationship between a sovereign King and His loyal subjects, who have been created for a certain purpose ("Kingship"). That purpose creates certain expectations but also fills the world and our lives with meaning. As such, God remembers and takes note of everything we do ("Remembrances"), and cares enough to provide a spiritual road map for us to follow, so we can derive the greatest possible good from our existence ("Shofar Blasts").

Once we have internalized these fundamental concepts – mission accomplished! We can then move on to asking God for forgiveness for our specific sins and shortcomings. It just wouldn't make sense to ask for forgiveness from a Being whose relationship to humanity is not understood and firmly established. We therefore spend Rosh Hashanah reciting prayers that help us place our relationship with God in its proper perspective, and only afterwards do we proceed to ask for forgiveness.

One final point: If we take the time on Rosh Hashanah to truly internalize these ideas – that there is a God; that this God willed us into existence for a certain purpose; that God takes notice and remembers all that we do and gives us the gift of the Torah to follow – then we will be more likely to live up to these ideals. No doubt, we will continue to make mistakes and even sin, but if we keep these principles in the front of our minds, we will sin less, since we are more focused on the purpose for our existence.

And so, during your Rosh Hashanah prayers, take notice of and make sure to reflect on *Malchiyot* (Kingship), *Zichronot* (Remembrances), and *Shofarot* (Trumpet Blasts). Contemplate these ideas, not only while you pray in synagogue, but think about them during the days which follow. Allow these basic concepts of Judaism to permeate your psyche and seep into your soul. As the Baal Shem Tov (1698–1760), the founder of the Chasidic movement, famously remarked: "You are where your thoughts are."

Question: What activities, during the course of your regular day, trigger the idea that God is a caring King who provides us with a path for our lives?

_____

_____

_____

_____

Day 27
Staying Connected

ONCE UPON A TIME, A PRINCE INFORMED HIS FATHER, THE King, that he was tired of being raised in the palace. He wanted more privacy from the constant attention and wanted to go undercover so he could live among his subjects. The King was reluctant to let his son, the heir to his throne, leave the protected cocoon in which he was raised, but the Prince was relentless. The King agreed to let him go but handed him a scroll reminding the Prince of his regal lineage, insisting that the son read it once in the morning upon arising and once at night before going to sleep. The Prince readily agreed and went on his way.

The King wrote letters to his son and eagerly anticipated his son's responses. The Prince responded to the King's letters and diligently reviewed the scroll twice each day. After a few weeks though he felt comfortable reading it before going to sleep only. After another few months, he opted to read it only once a week. After about a year, he ceased reading it at all.

When the King's letters started to go unanswered, he became concerned for his son's well-being. The King dispatched his top general, someone who had helped raise the Prince, to find out what was wrong. The general traveled among the people until he found the Prince's modest abode. He knocked on the door and was shocked to see a disheveled and gaunt man standing at the entrance. The young man was barely recognizable as the once healthy and vivacious Prince. The general approached to embrace the prince but the Prince pulled back claiming that he did not know the general and denied being a Prince.

The human mind has an acute ability to forget and to convince itself of alternative realities. It's amazing how easily we can forget who we are.

The final two commandments found at the end of the Torah are the mitzvot of *Hakhel* and writing a Torah scroll. *Hakhel*, meaning "assembly," was the mitzvah for the Jewish King to gather the entire nation – men, women, and children – and publicly read the Torah to all those assembled. The final commandment of the Torah is the mitzvah for each Jew to write a Torah scroll for themselves.

What is the significance of the fact that these are the *last* two commandments recorded in the Torah – both transmitted by Moshe on the day of his passing?

The Lubavitcher Rebbe explained that as long as the Jewish people remained in the desert, memories of the Sinai experience of revelation – when God gave the Torah to the people – remained fresh in their minds. Every day, the Manna descended from heaven sustaining the people. Miriam's well provided them with water, and God's cloud of glory and pillar of fire guided and protected the Jews by day and night. All of these supernatural experiences reinforced the Sinai experience, that special moment of nearness and intimacy with Hashem.

But as Moshe's life was drawing to an end, the Jewish people were about to leave that spiritual oasis in the wilderness – where they were surrounded by constant reminders of God's closeness and love. As they entered the land of Israel, the Jews were forced to undergo a maturation process. In the desert, their needs were provided for them, often in a miraculous fashion. In Israel however, there would be no more Manna falling from the heavens. Once they would enter the land of Israel, they would need to build homes, plant seeds, raise cattle, and plow the land. They would have to work to earn a living!

As these real-world struggles would begin to set in, it would be easier to forget about God. As the Jewish people would become absorbed into the whirlwind of day-to-day life, without the daily miracles to which they had been accustomed, the likelihood of neglecting their spiritual legacy and forgetting their Jewish origins became more real. Therefore, upon God's command, Moshe related these last two mitzvot of *Hakhel* and the writing of a Torah scroll, to help the Jews recreate the experience of Sinai in their new setting, in the land of Israel.

Perhaps even more so in our own time, we can easily feel like the Sinai experience is far from us. We don't have a King to convene the people and publicly read the Torah and most of us do not own our own Torah scrolls. Nevertheless, these two commandments are still relevant today because even if we no longer have the practice of *Hakhel*, we still gather to hear the Torah publicly read every Shabbat in synagogue. (We read from the Torah on Mondays and Thursdays as well.) And even if we don't have our own Torah scrolls, we can fulfill this commandment by purchasing and owning Jewish books. Having those books in our homes and studying from them whenever we can, enables us to continue what was started at Sinai when the Torah was first revealed. Hearing the Torah read publicly in synagogue and reading Jewish books in the privacy of our homes can help recreate the Sinai experience for our lives today.

Rabbi Joseph B. Soloveitchik explained that when we read the

Torah publicly, we place the Torah scroll on what is called a *bimah* – an elevated platform – because the public reading of the Torah is a reenactment of Sinai, which took place on a mountain. That is also why Rabbi Soloveitchik believed that people should face the *bimah* while the Torah is being read, because the Jews in synagogue today are like those who stood at Sinai facing the mountain as the Torah was given. The person reading the Torah is like Moshe coming down with the Torah, transmitting it to the people.

Similarly, when we study Torah privately, the experience of deepening our knowledge and connection to God also brings us back to that moment when the Torah was first revealed to our ancestors. Torah learning should therefore always feel fresh and new. Learning Torah, at any time, should be like receiving it for the very first time.

Just like our ancestors who entered Israel, we too have to work for a living. The days of the Manna falling from the heavens have passed, and we have so many demands on our time. Our professional ambitions, our bosses and clients with high expectations, and our commitments to our family and friends all exert tremendous pressure on our attention and focus. It feels like there's never enough time and it's just so easy to drift away from our life goals and spiritual aspirations.

Now – in the month of Elul – is the time to recommit ourselves to those goals through greater Torah study. Now is the time to hear the Torah read publicly and to learn more Torah privately because nothing returns us to Sinai and connects us more with Hashem than the study of His great wisdom. For Torah study is more than an intellectual exercise as the Zohar, one of the primary sources for Kabbalistic wisdom, teaches that "the Torah and God are totally one" (Zohar 1, 24a, 60a). Rabbi Schneur Zalman of Liadi explains this in the *Tanya* to mean that the Torah is more than just a glimmer of the Divine but "completely one with God Himself," meaning that God has so invested Himself in the Torah that He became one with it. Studying Torah is therefore not simply acquiring more information or knowledge. It is the process through which our souls become connected with the divine and immersed within the light of Hashem. The more we study, the more we will keep the Sinai experience alive and stay connected to our Source and remember who we truly are.

Question: What action(s) can you take in order to keep yourself feeling connected to Sinai? For example, praying more regularly, attending a weekly Torah class, or any other mitzvah that you can undertake on a regular basis.

_____

_____

_____

_____

Day 28
Our Father, Our King

ONE OF THE MOST FAMOUS AND STIRRING PARTS OF THE High Holiday service is the *Avinu Malkeinu* prayer, "Our Father, Our King." We recite this prayer every day from Rosh Hashanah until Yom Kippur (except on Shabbat) and to many, it is an emotional highlight of the Rosh Hashanah/Yom Kippur liturgy.

What makes the *Avinu Malkeinu* prayer so important? The prayer's significance is based on a story recorded in the Talmud (*Taanit* 25b) of a terrible drought which took place in the land of Israel during the times of the Mishnah. Since Israel was an agriculturally based society, the lack of rain made the Jewish community feel desperate. No rain could mean starvation. There were therefore all sorts of attempts on the part of the Jewish community to knock on heaven's door. One great rabbi after the next came forward with prayers to entreat God for rain, beseeching the Almighty for water. But all their supplications fell short.

Finally, the great Talmudic sage Rabbi Akiva – who only began to learn Torah at the age of forty – stepped forward and recited a simple prayer beginning with the words *Avinu Malkeinu*, "Our

Father, our King." The heavens opened, and it began to rain. The Jewish community in Israel was saved.

Although Rabbi Akiva's phrase sounds very simple, it is quite profound on the theological level, because it captures the two different aspects of our relationship with God: God as our parent and God as our King.

On one hand, like a parent, God is close to us and acts with compassion because He loves us. And from this perspective we have a day of judgment, not because God wants to nitpick and find fault with us but because, like a parent, God wants us to become the best version of ourselves. For that, a day of evaluation is necessary. On the other hand, God is also the King and Sovereign of the Universe and so He judges us – His loyal subjects.

Which is it though? What kind of relationship do we have with God? Is it the loving relationship of a parent to a child? Or is our relationship better described by the reverence of a subject to his ruler? Is God *Avinu* – our Father, or is He *Malkeinu* – our King and Sovereign?

The answer, of course, is both. We enjoy both aspects to our relationship with Hashem. God is both "our Father" – a loving parent, and "our King" – our sovereign leader.

There are different prayers that speak to each of these two aspects of our relationship with Hashem. The famous *Ashrei* prayer (Psalm 145), for example, speaks about the close and loving relationship we have with God as a benevolent and caring parent: "You open up Your hand, and satisfy the desire of every living thing" (v. 16); "God is close to all who call upon Him" (v. 18); "God protects all those who love Him" (v. 20); "God supports all the fallen ones and straightens all the bent" (v. 14). And there are more such verses in the *Ashrei* prayer depicting our personal and intimate relationship with God.

But before we say the *Ashrei* every day, we also recite the *Yehi Kavod* prayer – a collection of biblical verses which speak about God as King and Ruler of the Universe. Verses such as "High above all nations is God, above the heavens in His glory" (113:2–4); "God has established His throne in the heavens, and His kingdom reigns over all" (Psalms 103:19); "God shall reign for all eternity" (Exodus 15:18). This prayer depicts Hashem as the transcendental King and Ruler of the Universe. This prayer, the *Yehi Kavod*, is therefore recited immediately before *Ashrei*, in order to show both sides to our relationship with the One and Only God.

This is the dual nature of our relationship with God. He is both a King who rules over us and a loving parent who cares for us. We begin the *Avinu Malkeinu* with God as "our Father" because we want to first appeal to the aspect of our relationship with God that is a loving parent, a God who longs for His children to return after they have strayed. But God is also our sovereign King who we revere and to whom we acknowledge we could have been more loyal subjects throughout the year.

Perhaps that is what opened the gates of heaven and caused the rain to fall when Rabbi Akiva came forward with this simple but profound prayer. For the words *Avinu Malkeinu* – "Our Father, Our King" – epitomize the true nature of our twofold relationship with God – a king deserving of obedience and loyalty and a caring parent who desires only love and goodness for His children.

Question: Do you think of God more as a parent or a ruler? How can you strengthen the other perception?

_____

_____

_____

_____

Day 29
The Message of the *Shofar*

WHEN RABBI LEVI YITZCHAK OF BERDICHEV (1740–1810), one of the greatest and most pious Chasidic leaders of his day, sought a *baal tokeya* (*shofar* blower) for his synagogue, people came from far and wide dreaming to be selected by the grand rabbi. As Reb Levi, as he was affectionately referred to, interviewed each candidate, he asked each person what thoughts were going through their mind as they blew the *shofar*. Some shared they were thinking about the many *halachot* (Jewish laws) pertaining to the mitzvah, while others said they meditated on the mystical ideas underlying the sounds of the *shofar*. However, one simple Jew answered differently: "I have a daughter who has not yet succeeded in finding a husband. As I blow the *shofar*, I think of my daughter and pray she finds the right husband and that I have enough money to feed my family."

Of all the candidates, Reb Levi chose this simple Jew to be his *shofar* blower because, for our prayers and *shofar* blasts to be favorably received by the Almighty, honesty and sincerity are critical. The *shofar* – which is considered the ultimate prayer – is beyond words, and is therefore ideally sounded by someone who is genuine and pious.

What else should we know about the *shofar* as we approach Rosh Hashanah?

The *shofar* is sounded on Rosh Hashanah and there is a custom to blow it every day of the month of Elul. It occupies a very important part of Jewish tradition and plays a central role in how we Jews celebrate the Jewish New Year. The *shofar* also carries great historical significance. The *shofar* was sounded in times of war to call Jewish soldiers to battle. It was heard at Sinai when God revealed the Torah to the Jewish people, and it was also sounded to appoint a Jewish king, which is what we are doing on Rosh Hashanah – coronating God as our King.

Besides these historical moments, though, there are also a number of interesting *halachot* (Jewish laws) pertaining to the *shofar*. These details, which might seem insignificant at first glance, reveal some of the critical values and ideals that are important to consider at this time of the year.

For example, the Talmud explains that the *shofar* has to be *kafuf*, which literally means "bent over." The *shofar* should not be perfectly upright, a symbol that when we pray, we too should appear before God humbly and modestly, or "bent over" as it were – understanding who we are in relation to our Creator. We raise our voices before God in prayer, but we don't come in blasting away. Like the *shofar*, we appear *kafuf*, a little bent over – without any arrogance or pride.

Another interesting Jewish law mentioned in the Talmud is the concept of *nistak larko pasul* – which means that the *shofar* cannot be split down the middle. If the *shofar* is cracked in this way, it is disqualified. Similarly, when we come before the Almighty on the High Holidays, we too cannot be "split down the middle." We need to project a clear message with clarity and conviction. We need to articulate our goals and vision for the coming year. What is it that we want this Rosh Hashanah? What kind of people do we want to be? What defines our relationship with God and with one another? We must endeavor to articulate our goals for the coming year and how we plan to get there – our message can't be wishy-washy. As the Talmud teaches in regard to the *shofar*, we can't afford to be split down the middle where we are sometimes one way and sometimes another.

One last *halachah*: According to one opinion in the Talmud, it is permissible for the mouth of the *shofar* to be plated with gold. However, the *shofar* is disqualified if the gold alters the sound. In other words, there's no problem with having some gold on a *shofar* – unless the gold changes the tone (which is the primary purpose of the *shofar*).

We all have messages we want to impart to our families, co-workers, and friends. If the "gold," or the money, changes the message or it starts to change us, then we have a problem. Since generally we want the gold so much, we are tempted and often become willing to alter our message in life. We might feel pressured to say or do something or compromise our values in some way to make that extra dollar. Please do not misunderstand me, there's nothing wrong with pursuing "the gold." We all have to earn a living, support our families, and donate to charity. Judaism never looked down on money or financial success, nor does Jewish tradition elevate poverty into a religious ideal. But we must remember that money or financial success is only a means to living a just, upright, and spiritual life. Money is just a tool, a device for something greater – never an end in itself. Therefore, we can have some gold on the *shofar*, but it becomes disqualified when the gold starts changing the sound or the message.

We must all "bring home the gold," but as we approach the High

Holidays, let us make sure it does not stop us from becoming our best selves.

Question: What is it that you really want in the coming year that you can think about and pray for when the *shofar* is being sounded?

_____

_____

_____

_____

Day 30
Breath and Honey
Erev Rosh Hashanah

HOW MANY TIMES HAVE WE BEEN TOLD TO "TAKE A DEEP breath"? We've also heard the comment that someone "takes our breath away" or perhaps we've experienced a gasp or shortness of breath when we feel surprised or scared. What is happening with our respiratory system in those moments of great drama?

Noted pulmonologist Dr. Steven Thau explained that while our lungs have enormous capacity – when they are not physically active, they only operate at ten percent capacity or even less. The amount of breath we need is determined by the physical activities in which we are engaged. And so, at those times when our system is surprised, inspired, or scared, it takes a moment for the brain to send a message to the diaphragm that more air is needed or that adrenaline needs to be released. That is precisely when we feel that sensation of being breathless – when our bodies hit the pause button to make sure it adjusts to what the senses are experiencing.

Breath takes on a major role on Rosh Hashanah. Although we generally refer to the Jewish New Year as "Rosh Hashanah" – the beginning or the head of the year – the Torah refers to this holiday as *Yom Teruah*, "the day of blasting" (Numbers 29:1), referring to the mitzvah to use our breath to sound the *shofar*, a ram's horn, on this special day.

Interestingly, each time we blow the *shofar* in synagogue, we afterwards recite the Hebrew phrase: *ha-yom harat olam*, "today is the birthday of the world," referring to the Jewish tradition that Adam and Eve, the first people to walk this earth, were created on Rosh Hashanah. But why does the prayer book connect the *shofar* with the birthday of humankind? What does the use of our breath to blow a ram's horn have to do with the creation of the human race?

Rabbi Jonathan Eybeschutz (eighteenth century) wrote that the significance of the *shofar* goes all the way back to the Garden of Eden. The Torah tells us that when God created man out of the dust of the ground, "He blew into his nostrils the spirit of life, and man became a living being" (Genesis 2:7). It was God's breath that transformed man from a lifeless form to a spiritual entity. And so, on Rosh Hashanah – the anniversary of the day God created man with His breath – we observe the one mitzvah that requires us to use our breath to create something, in this case a sound from a ram's horn. By sounding the *shofar*, we begin our year by mimicking God's most enduring and creative act. The *shofar* is therefore the ultimate reminder of our creative capacity.

What do we want to create this year? How are we going to use our breath, our feet, our arms, our eyes? How are we going to direct the beautiful gifts God has given to us – the gift of our creation, the gift of life? If the worldwide pandemic has taught us anything, it is a greater appreciation for the gift of life, something we so often take for granted. What good will we do with our lives in the coming year?

Another important theme of Rosh Hashanah is expressed by

the well-known custom to dip an apple in some honey, expressing our hope and prayer for a sweet new year to come. But there's something deeper behind this practice. The Hebrew word for "honey" is *devash*, which is spelled *dalet, vet, shin*. The *gematria* or the numerical equivalent of the word *devash* is the same as the phrase *Av Ha-Rachamim*, which means "O Father of Compassion." Dipping the apple in the honey symbolizes more than the wish for a sweet year. We are invoking God's compassion. We are turning to God and saying that no matter how independent or advanced we moderns have become, we are still just simple mortals in need of God's love and compassion. As we approach Rosh Hashanah and Yom Kippur, we acknowledge that however intellectually sophisticated we may be, we don't know everything and we remain dependent on God's mercy and kindness. That is our mindset on Rosh Hashanah: God is the King, and we are His humble servants.

Thus, step one – symbolized by the apple and honey – is to come before God with a sense of humility and modesty, with a sincere asking of Hashem to be compassionate with us. Step two – embodied by the mitzvah to use our breath to blow the *shofar* – is to demonstrate our commitment to use all our God-given strengths and talents to deepen our connection with God in the coming year. The sounds of the *shofar* help us recall God's original creation of man through Hashem's breath and how we are now using our breath to create something new. In doing so, we pledge to God to use every breath and every gift He has given us for the greatest possible purpose – utilizing the mitzvot to better ourselves and the world around us.

May our demonstration of humility and our commitment to using all our gifts for their greatest good serve as a merit for a *K'tiva V'chatima Tova* – that may we all be written and inscribed into the book of life for a year of good health, joy, meaning, and purpose.

Question: What is one talent you possess and how can you better channel that gift towards a holy or communal goal?

_____

_____

_____

_____

Day 31
Working with What You've Got
First Day Rosh Hashanah

ONE OF MY FRIENDS IS AN ACCOMPLISHED CHESS PLAYER. After years of studying the game, he was presented with the opportunity to play a game of chess against a bona fide chess grandmaster. The two players sat down and, after a few moves, the grandmaster said to my friend, "It looks like you are trying to capture my queen. Why are you doing this?"

My friend answered, "The queen is the most powerful piece on the board. If I can capture your queen, I'd have a better chance of winning." The grandmaster looked down at the board, then back up at his opponent. He reached down, took the queen from the board, and handed it over. The grandmaster then asked, "Are there any other impediments preventing you from winning?" His younger opponent thought for a moment and pointed to the two rooks. Once again, the grandmaster removed these two critical pieces and handed them to my friend.

"Anything else?" he asked. By this time, my friend was too embarrassed to just ask for the king, or for the knights, or the bishops, so he just shook his head and said no.

"Good," said the grandmaster, "no more impediments." And with the remaining pieces, the grandmaster proceeded to demolish his young opponent.

We all have obstacles and impediments, but we also have gifts and blessings to meet those challenges. Without a queen and two rooks, most of us would throw up our hands and give up, but a chess grandmaster can see other possibilities and use what he has to win the game. In a sense, we're all in that situation, because we all have challenges, and we all have gifts. The question is: Do we use one to compensate for the other?

At age fifty-seven, Rahamim Melamed-Cohen had a great life. He was the father of six beautiful children and a proud grandfather, held a PhD in Special Education, served in a senior role in the Israeli Ministry of Education, and had authored two critically acclaimed books. One day he began to feel weakness in his left shoulder. As he was reciting the Kiddush on Shabbat evening, the Kiddush cup shook, and the wine spilled. Dr. Melamed-Cohen and his wife Elisheva visited numerous specialists until one doctor finally told him he had amyotrophic lateral sclerosis (ALS), better known as Lou Gehrig's Disease. The doctor outlined the fatal course of the disease. His muscles would slowly stop working and he would become paralyzed. He would ultimately be dependent on people for everything until even his lungs would stop working. "You have three to five years to live," the doctor told him.

That was over twenty years ago. Since that time, Rahamim has become completely paralyzed and can only communicate through a program which tracks his eye movement. Yet Rahamim begins every day by praying and studying Torah. He continues to go to work, where he is consulted by people throughout the world on a myriad of educational issues. He has mastered Photoshop, which allows him to paint with his eyes. He has publicly debated Israeli advocates of euthanasia and most incredibly, since his illness, Rahamim Melamed-Cohen has authored eight new books, including a book of advice for people suffering from chronic or terminal illness.

How does a person whose life is so profoundly compromised function so highly? Because Rahamim Melamed-Cohen can see the abilities and qualities he does have, while working around what he doesn't. Like the chess grandmaster, he can see possibilities others might not notice.

In the biblical book of Kings (part of Hebrew Scripture) a woman approached the prophet Elisha in total desperation. She had just lost her husband and the family was in such debt the creditors were coming to take her two sons as slaves. When she cried out for help, Elisha responded: *Mah yeish lach ba'bayit*, "What do you have in the house?" (2 Kings 4:2). Elisha did not ask: "Do you have anything in the house to help you," but instead he said, "What *do* you have?" There's got to be something you already have that we can work with.

I shared this idea with a student who was furloughed at the beginning of the COVID-19 pandemic. He was very down about losing his job and being unemployed but at the same time he is a beloved and popular person in our community. And so, I suggested he work his connections. He was embarrassed to do so but his popularity was the blessing he had to work with. There was another MJE participant who felt isolated in her apartment in Manhattan also due to the pandemic, but I knew she was close with her parents, so I suggested she go back home and be with her family because that was the blessing she had in her life.

Mah yeish lach ba'bayit, what do you already have in your house?

What qualities and talents do you possess that can help you succeed in your careers, in your relationships, and in your spiritual growth?

During this time of year, it's appropriate to ask ourselves: Are we sufficiently using the gifts and resources we have at our disposal or do we allow our challenges to keep us from being our best selves?

I remember one time I invited someone to attend my Basic Judaism class, and he said, "Thanks, Rabbi, but it's not for me. I won't be able to follow the class since I didn't even go to Hebrew School." I answered him, "This isn't an advanced Talmud class, it's just Basic Judaism. You're a smart guy and you'll figure it out. If you can apply your gift of intelligence in other areas of your life, then why not here?" Someone else who I was encouraging to learn to read Hebrew said to me, "I'm already thirty-two. If I haven't learned it by now, it's not going to happen." I said, "Wow, I never knew there was a cutoff age for learning Hebrew. Rabbi Akiva, arguably the greatest Talmudic sage, was forty when he began!"

We so often define ourselves according to our limitations rather than our possibilities. Some of the greatest scholars and leaders in the Jewish community today were not raised with much Judaism. In the class that I teach at RIETS, Yeshiva University's rabbinical school, I had one student who had converted to Judaism just a few years earlier and he became a fully ordained rabbi – from convert to rabbi in eight years.

Because for whatever we don't have, we've got something else to use. Someone may not have the height in a basketball game, but they've got speed and energy. Maybe we can't always provide our bosses with the exact work product they want, but we come to work with such a positive attitude that everyone else wants us around. We may not be able to open a Jewish text and understand what it says, but we have a deep curiosity and drive that someone who can easily read the text is perhaps lacking. Our parents may not have raised us to observe Shabbat, but maybe because we chose it ourselves, we are even more excited about it!

We all have impediments and flaws, but we were given talents and strengths to compensate. The only question is which do we pay more attention to – our flaws or our talents? The challenges or the strengths?

The great Rambam explained that the purpose of the *shofar* that we sound on Rosh Hashanah is to wake us up from our slumber. It's easy to get distracted by our surroundings and everyday responsibilities, and not always so easy to "wake up" and do an honest assessment: what are our impediments and, more importantly, what strengths can we use to overcome them? The *shofar* is sounded to wake us up to the great blessings we have right before us. We turn to God and we say, "Yes, we have weaknesses, but this year we will use the strengths You blessed us with to compensate for those limitations, so we can fulfill our life mission and reach our spiritual potential."

Let's work with what we've got and use "what we have in our house" to elevate ourselves and the world around us.

Question: Identify one unique gift or talent you possess and one real challenge in your life. How can you use the gift to meet the challenge?

_____

_____

_____

_____

Day 32
Warming Others
Second Day Rosh Hashanah

THERE WAS A JEW NAMED YANKEL WHO OWNED A BAKERY in Crown Heights. Yankel survived the concentration camps and eventually emigrated to the United States. One time after he settled in America, someone asked him how he was able to survive the camps and come out alive when so many others had perished.

Yankel said he attributed his survival to one particular incident that took place when he was a teenager on the train to the camps. The Nazis would transport Jews in box cars and sometimes they would leave the trains unattended overnight, even for days, without providing food or water. And of course, there were no blankets to keep anyone warm.

Yankel found himself in a box car filled with fellow Jews being taken to Auschwitz. Night came and it was freezing cold. The Nazis left the train sitting overnight. Sitting next to Yankel was an older Jew, a beloved gentleman who Yankel recognized from his hometown. The elderly man was shivering from head to toe, and he looked awful.

"I wrapped my arms around him," Yankel described. "I began to warm him up by rubbing his arms and legs, his neck and face. I begged him all night to be strong and to hang on, telling him it would be better in the morning. Somehow, I kept the old man warm, but I was exhausted and I myself was freezing. My fingers were numb, but I didn't stop rubbing heat unto this man's body."

Yankel continued to describe what happened: "The hours dragged on slowly, but finally the night passed and the morning came. The sun began to shine, and I felt a little warmth in the box car. Some sunlight entered and I looked around. To my utter horror, all I could see were frozen bodies. There was a deathly silence. Nobody in the car made it through the night. Only two people survived the night – me and the old man. The old man survived because someone kept him warm, and I survived because I was warming someone else."

One of the secrets of Judaism is that when you warm another person, you remain warm yourself. We might think that when we go out of our way for someone else, we're only doing it for them. But we're also doing it for ourselves.

The Talmud teaches *ner la-echad ner le-meah*, "a candle for one is a candle for a hundred people" (*Shabbat* 122a). When we create light for another person, we bring light to ourselves, transforming the lives of everyone around us. The same applies to our spiritual growth and to Torah study: when we share wisdom with others, we ourselves benefit. As the Rambam taught: "The Sages said: 'Much wisdom have I learned from my masters, more than that from my colleagues, but from my disciples – more than from all of them combined.' Just as a small tree kindles a big one, so does a small disciple sharpen the mind of his master, for through [the student's] questions he brings forth from him a beautified wisdom" ("Laws of Torah Study" 5:13). As I can testify from personal experience, when a teacher gives a class, it doesn't just benefit the students. Sharing knowledge and wisdom with others also enables the teacher to better understand and appreciate the material he or she is teaching.

Giving to others – whether it's helping to keep someone else alive physically or inspiring another spiritually – does at least as much for the person giving as it does for the one receiving. May we all merit in the coming year to take care of someone else, to extend ourselves on behalf of another human being. Who do you know that can use some extra attention this year? Someone who can use a donation or a loan to get them through a hard time? Who, in your orbit, can benefit from the warmth and wisdom you have to give? Remember that in the end, the love and embrace you offer others will bring you at least as much love and warmth in return.

Question: Who do you know that you can help with a donation, a loan, or a job to get them through a hard time? If there is no such person in your circle, choose one organization that helps others to which you can donate and/or volunteer.

_____

_____

_____

_____

Day 33
Fasting after Feasting
Tzom Gedaliah

TODAY IS THE FIRST DAY AFTER THE MAJESTY AND AWE OF Rosh Hashanah, but besides for being the first day after the Jewish New Year, it has a unique identity all its own. Today is known as the "Fast of Gedaliah," named for the Jewish leader Gedaliah ben Achikam. After the Babylonians, led by Nebuchadnezzar, conquered the land of Israel and destroyed the First Temple in Jerusalem in 586 BCE, most of the Jewish community in Israel was killed or exiled. A minority of Jews were permitted to remain in Israel, and Nebuchadnezzar appointed Gedaliah as their governor. Several years later, Gedaliah was assassinated, and the last remaining Jews were forced into exile. The Fast of Gedaliah therefore represents the last of the Jews being sent into exile.

I always wondered though, what's the connection this fast day has to the High Holiday season? Some joke that after all the eating we do on Rosh Hashanah, the Jewish Sages thought a fast on the day after would be a good idea! On a more serious note, though, this fast day seems completely disconnected. We have just emerged from the spiritual high of Rosh Hashanah and today is the third day of *Aseret Yemei Teshuvah*, of the Ten Days of Repentance leading up to Yom Kippur. We're supposed to be trying to get closer to God during this time. Why do we observe the Fast of Gedaliah right now, when it seems to be historically and thematically disconnected?

The Kabbalists teach us that when we sin, we are, in a sense, sending ourselves into exile because our natural state is to be one with God. Rabbi Schneur Zalman of Liadi, author of the great work called the *Tanya*, wrote that each one of us has a *nefesh elokit* – a Godly soul which, in its natural state, is connected to God. We are created in a way that is naturally pure and good, inexorably linked to our Divine source. Sin – which has the effect of distancing ourselves from God – is therefore considered a deviation, sending our Godly soul into exile.

That is why the Hebrew term for "repentance" is *teshuvah*, which literally means "return." Returning implies that, at an earlier point, we were already there! But when were we there? The answer is we were always "there" because that is metaphysically the way we were formed. Our souls were created in a state that was and continues to be spiritually connected to God. Therefore, when we do something against the laws of the Torah – against God's will – we're doing something unnatural, sending ourselves from our familiar place of connectedness into a foreign place of exile.

Perhaps that is why we observe the Fast of Gedaliah right after Rosh Hashanah. For the Fast of Gedaliah represents the last remnant of the Jewish people being sent into exile during the Babylonian reign. And at this time of year, when we consider the mistakes we've made in the past year, we reflect on how, through our sins, we too have exiled our souls, and ultimately how we yearn to return to God.

That is what we're trying to do on an individual level, but the

Fast of Gedaliah inspires us to also think about this on the national level. At this time of year, the entire Jewish people – as a nation – are also trying to pull themselves out of exile. Today, as we fast and commemorate the last remnant of surviving Jews who were sent into exile by the Babylonians, we ask ourselves what we can do as a nation to be closer to God.

Remembering that our natural and default state – both as individuals and as a nation – is to be connected with God, and that it is only our sins that have created distance, can inspire us to do what is necessary to close the spiritual gap and return to God. Let's use this time to do exactly that, and in doing so merit to see the rebuilding of the Temple and the return of our souls from exile.

Question: Are the Jewish fast days part of your spiritual schedule? If not, what new fast day resonates with you that you could observe in the coming year?

_____

_____

_____

_____

Day 34
Desensitization

AS I MENTIONED IN THE INTRODUCTION, DURING THE COVID pandemic, I started a WhatsApp group, so that I could stay in touch with my students on a daily basis. I called the WhatsApp group "Beyond the Instant," after the title of my first book – to provide some spiritual inspiration and encouragement to the many MJE participants. I was enjoying sharing the Torah messages each morning. What I loved most was that the group was interactive. I could share an idea and my students would respond with questions and thoughts of their own. There was a sense of togetherness fostered by lively discussions about Judaism. The group has grown to close to 500 followers, it inspired the writing of this very book, and to this day I continue to share words of Torah each and every morning. God bless technology!

But along with the great gift of technology comes some real challenges. One day, someone posted an obscene pornographic picture on the group chat. It was, to say the least, upsetting. It was disturbing – not only because the image itself was so distasteful – but because the group had come together to be positively inspired in growing closer to God and Judaism. Yet on that day, it was defiled with inappropriate content. Sadly, I had to shut down the interactive nature of the group to keep it a safe space.

Today's world is blessed with incredible advances in technology, science, and medicine. The internet offers amazing opportunities for growth, but it comes with risks. One of those risks is desensitization. We live in a society that constantly exposes us to content that can be hurtful and degrading and it's so easy to fall into the trap of thinking that these things are normal.

For most of us, technology is inseparable from our lives. The first thing we do upon arising is check our phones, and it's often the last thing we do before going to sleep. These devices have made it possible to build and maintain friendships, search for jobs at the click of a button, and find paths for intellectual and spiritual growth that didn't exist for most of human history. But in today's high-tech world, it is also easy to access and circulate content that distracts us from our mission in life. And in some cases, as with the disturbing image posted on the WhatsApp chat, the content not only distracts us from our higher purpose, but it can prevent us from attaining our higher goals of spirituality and moral goodness.

Our surroundings have a profound impact on us. The people around us, the images to which we are exposed, and the general society more broadly, influence our sensibilities and our sensitivities. Of course, we all have free will to think and behave as we wish, but the environment in which we operate – as well as the people with whom we associate – affect the way we think and ultimately behave.

The great Rambam wrote about this very practically: "It is natural for a man's character and actions to be influenced by his friends and associates and for him to follow the local norms of behavior. Therefore, he should associate with the righteous and be constantly in the company of the wise, so as to learn from their deeds. Conversely, he should keep away from the wicked who walk in darkness, so as not to learn from their deeds" ("Laws of Character Traits" 6:1).

This is why our Sages teach that one should try to associate with people of good moral character. Rambam explains that there is actually a mitzvah to spend time with sages and their students in order to learn from their ways. By surrounding ourselves with people of scholarship and spirituality, we will be positively influenced in our own path of growth and enlightenment.

Rambam quotes a verse from the Torah, "and you shall cleave to Him" (Deuteronomy 10:20), a reference to connecting to God. But as Rambam asks: "Is it really possible to cleave to God?" After all, God doesn't have a body or a physical presence of any kind. If that's the case, then how can we cleave to Him? Rather, the Torah is teaching us to find individuals who are connected to God or who represent God in some way, and attach ourselves to those people, for they will help us grow in the best possible way.

Similarly, the Sages teach: *oy la-rasha oy le-shechaino*, "Woe to a wicked person and woe to his neighbor" (*Avot De-Rabbi Nathan* 1.9). We might say to ourselves: "What's the big deal if my neighbor or my friend acts in a lowly manner or does bad things from time to time? After all, nobody's perfect." The Rabbis are teaching us that at the end of the day, the people we're surrounded by are the people who influence us. As much as we like to think of ourselves as independent thinkers, to a large degree we are products of our environment. We are positively impacted by positive stimuli and negatively impacted by negative stimuli. And so, if we surround ourselves with people who are interested in learning and growing, then we will grow as a result. Conversely, if we surround ourselves with those possessing baser motives – although we may not always realize it – we too will be dragged down with them. If, for example, we find that we have gravitated to someone who routinely speaks ill of others, or who speaks in a crass manner, we should minimize the time we spend with them unless, of course, the person is open to change. The concern is we become desensitized to those behaviors, and without realizing it we begin to adopt those ways of speaking ourselves.

This is not to say one should simply abandon a friend who is behaving in the wrong way. That would be insensitive and not the way a good friend should behave. As we discussed on Day 14 ("If You See Something Say Something"), a good friend points out their colleague's wrongdoing and tries to help them improve their character and behavior. This must be done in a sensitive manner and in a way that reflects your true motivation – the love you have for your friend and for their well-being.

However, if you see your friend is not open to change, then staying close with such an individual will only bring you down. It's easy to think we can expose ourselves to certain people or certain content or visual images and not be affected – that somehow, we're immune and we can rise above it unscathed. We can't always control who our coworkers are, or what our neighbors do. But we can control how we spend our free time and who we associate with "after hours." Are we seeking out friends, mentors, teachers, and even romantic partners, who are interested in spiritual growth and refinement? Are we guiding the direction of our lives, or just following what everyone else is doing?

Modern society has bestowed innumerable benefits upon us, and we must thank God for those incredible gifts. To utilize those gifts for our own self growth – to become the best version of ourselves – we must surround ourselves with the right people, the right influences, and always, with positive images.

Question: What is one positive way you use technology and one negative way? How would you build on the former and cut down on the latter?

_____

_____

_____

_____

Day 35
The Power to Change

ZAC CLARK WAS A NORMAL YOUNG TWENTY-SOMETHING until one day, he was diagnosed with a brain tumor. After his surgery he became addicted to painkillers and his life spiraled out of control: he got a DUI, his wife left him, and he was arrested. Zac was in and out of rehab and it was far from clear whether he would ever live a normal life again, or if he would die from an overdose, like so many others before him. Yet somehow Zac was able to become successfully rehabilitated. Even more impressive, he used his past demons to help others. Once he got clean, Zac co-founded a drug rehab center which has helped countless other people become sober.

Why do we begin the holiest night of the year, the night of Yom Kippur, with *Kol Nidrei*? The *Kol Nidrei* prayer is essentially an annulling of any vows or promises we may have made throughout the year which we did not fulfill. It seems strange that we should focus on something so technical and esoteric as the annulling of vows. On a night devoted to the atonement of our sins and our greatest connection with God, why do we focus on something so rote and mechanical?

Judaism views our words as paramount. The way we speak and

the promises we make are of supreme importance. In our daily prayers we say: "Blessed be He who spoke, and the world came into being," reflecting the Jewish belief that God created the world with words – using the medium of speech. Through speech, we too can create new realities and, like God, we can use our words to create, to lift people up or, God forbid, to bring others down. So, the first reason for reciting *Kol Nidrei* on the holiest night of the year is to demonstrate – both to ourselves and to God – how seriously we take the words we use.

But there's a deeper reason why we begin Yom Kippur by annulling our vows. Rabbi Joseph Soloveitchik suggests that we begin with *Kol Nidrei* because that is exactly the way *teshuvah* works. *Teshuvah*, which literally means to "return" to God after we have sinned, is an otherworldly gift. Because in this world, when we do something wrong – we insult someone, we steal something – it can't be undone. We can apologize for insulting a friend or return the money we've stolen and vow to never repeat the bad behavior, but we can never take back what we've done. No matter how bad we feel or how many times we apologize, the negative remarks are still out there. The hurt we caused might subside, but it never goes away completely. We can't undo the sins that we have committed.

The Talmud, however, tells us that not only can sins be undone but they can be transformed. If we do *teshuvah* or "return" out of fear, that *teshuvah* can transform our intentional sins into accidental sins, as though we committed that sin by accident, and if we repent out of the motivation of love, then our act of *teshuvah* can transform our sins into merits (*Yoma* 86b).

But how is that possible? In the physical world in which we live, once something is done, we can't take it back. We live our physical lives within the confines of time and space, and within those constraints, we can't take back our sins. For this reason, the Sages view *teshuvah* as a gift from another world. In our physical world, limited by time and space, *teshuvah* makes no sense. But it is not of this world – *teshuvah* is a gift from another, more spiritual realm.

All of this is symbolized in the *Kol Nidrei*. I took a vow, or I made a promise which I failed to keep. I said something which was inappropriate. I took something which didn't belong to me. I may be ashamed and embarrassed about it, but on a physical plane, as much as I'd like to, I can't take it back. *Teshuvah* tells us otherwise. *Teshuvah* says we can take it back.

We *can* change reality. As far as God is concerned, once we have engaged in a sincere and proper *teshuvah* – once we recognize where we have gone wrong, express our remorse, and resolve to do better for the future (what Rabbi Leo Jung called the three R's: recognition of sin, remorse, and resolution to do better in the future) – we can change the past and transform it for the future.

And so, that vow or promise we made which we never kept – it's as though it never happened. Not only that, but if the *teshuvah* is motivated by love, then we can take the negative energy of that unfulfilled promise and convert it into something positive. Our past shortcomings thus become reinvigorated and allow us to live a completely different life, because the Torah believes so deeply in the power of change and personal transformation. Just as Zac Clark used his own past addiction to help others confront their challenges, we too can change and even elevate the past. This is why Reish Lakish, a reformed gangster turned Talmudic sage, was able to say with all honesty and sincerity that if someone does repentance from a place of love, his sins are transformed into merits.

God believes in our ability to make real change in our lives, and so He gifts us this treasure from another world, the power of *teshuvah*. May we use it wisely.

Question: What past misdeed, failing, or personality flaw can you now use to help other people?

_____

_____

_____

_____

Day 36
You Can Run,
But You Can't Hide

THE GREAT SAGE, RABBI SHIMON BAR YOCHAI, TELLS OF A parable involving a boat that is beginning to sink. The men and women aboard the boat are frantically scurrying around, looking for the cause of the sinking ship. Finally, they find one of the passengers drilling a hole in the floor of his room. The other passengers begin screaming at the man, demanding he cease his drilling. The man responded, "Why do you care? I'm only drilling under my seat – not yours!" (*Vayikra Rabbah* 4:6).

The lesson of the parable is clear: we're all in the same boat and must see our lives as inexorably connected with one another. What is our responsibility to *each other* during the High Holiday season? As individuals, we take advantage of this time on the Jewish calendar to right our wrongs, apologize to our friends, and engage in the process of *teshuvah* – spiritually returning to God and to the deepest part of our selves. But what about those around us? What is our obligation to our fellow Jews – and to our fellow non-Jews – when it comes to their spiritual journey?

On Yom Kippur afternoon, in the *Mincha* service we read *Sefer Yonah*, the book about the biblical prophet Jonah. In this book of Hebrew Scripture, God comes to Jonah and tells him to travel to the city of Nineveh and encourage their citizens to repent of their corrupt ways. What is interesting about God's command to Jonah, though, is that Nineveh – the capital of the ancient Assyrian Empire – was *not* a Jewish city. Although there were no Jews living there, God wanted Jonah to embark on this long and onerous journey and help them improve their ethical conduct.

Jonah, however, was not interested in the mission. He did not want to take on the responsibility and so, he flees to the city of Tarshish, in the exact opposite direction. When Tarshish isn't far enough, Jonah boards a boat to sail across the Mediterranean Sea. Yet, God keeps following Jonah, continually reminding him of his responsibility to improve the conduct of the people of Nineveh. Famously, the prophet gets thrown overboard and is swallowed up by a giant fish (or possibly a whale), but still refuses to get involved. Jonah remains stubborn the whole time, but God keeps trailing after him, teaching him – and all of us – that we can never escape our mission in life.

Often, we feel the urge to escape. We want to run in the opposite direction and flee from our own life purpose. But deep down we know we were created for a higher purpose and that purpose catches up with us eventually. You can run but you can't hide.

The larger theme of Jonah, though, has to do with our responsibility to our fellow human beings. On the High Holidays, the primary concern is with improving our own character, mending our own flaws, and reconnecting ourselves to God. But we must also be concerned with the spiritual and ethical growth of other people. We can't simply go about our own spiritual development while ignoring everyone else's.

This is a difficult concept for us to accept in modern society. In Western culture particularly, we are taught to stay out of other people's business, especially when it comes to religion and ethics. We generally take a more *laissez-faire* attitude when it comes to other people's lifestyle. The motto is: "live and let live." Religion is a personal matter and it not our place to interfere in other people's lives. Also, as outsiders, we can never truly know where someone else stands in their spiritual connection and devotion.

At the same time, if we truly felt connected to other people, if we really cared about other people's welfare – Jewish or not – it should bother us if someone is disconnected from their Creator or if they are not living up to their spiritual potential. We never want to come off as judgmental or "holier than thou," but we can inspire our fellow human beings in a positive way, not by preaching, but through leading by example. Every parent knows that children take their parent's actions much more seriously than their words. The same is true for people of any age. If we want to ignite a passion for Judaism and Godliness and inspire greater ethical conduct in the people around us, then we have to demonstrate that passion in our own behavior. What we say matters much less than what we do. And what we do can motivate other people, whose lives *should* matter to us.

The Talmud famously teaches that each Jew is responsible or is really a guarantor for every other Jew (*Sanhedrin* 27b). We are responsible for each other, not just in a physical sense, but spiritually as well. Feeling that sense of responsibility means caring about and helping our friends improve their relationship with God, so together we can all move closer to living a higher ethical ideal.

So, while Yom Kippur is certainly a time for our own personal growth, the book of Jonah reminds us of our responsibility to engage those around us and do what we can to inspire others in their religious and ethical growth – so they too can lead their best possible lives. A good friend isn't just someone to have fun with but is also that person who helps their colleagues become the very best version of themselves. And so, as we approach the holiest day of the year, let's remain mindful, not only of our own spiritual growth, but of our friends and family as well. Remember, we're all in the same boat.

Question: Who, in your circle of friends, could use some spiritual encouragement and how can you respectfully engage and direct them towards what they need?

_____

_____

_____

_____

Day 37
Living as Angels

IN 2015, THERE WAS A JEWISH WOMAN FROM BEVERLY HILLS who traveled to Israel with her family, rented a suite in a beautiful hotel in Herzliya, and requested an ocean view. When they arrived, the dining room had already closed for the night, so they decided to order in room service. A young Israeli waiter entered her hotel room, set down the food, and before he left, said to the family:

"My name is Barak. If you need anything else, please do not hesitate to call."

The woman's husband calls him back. "Your name is Barak?"

"Yes," the waiter answered.

"By chance, is your mother's name Aurna?"

"Yes," the waiter again answered.

"Did you fight in the Gaza War last summer?"

"Yes. How did you know?"

"Because I got a call to pray for a Barak ben Aurna. We had your name on our refrigerator door in California. Our family prayed for your safety every day. Each and every day we prayed for Barak ben Aurna – may he have a *refuah sheleimah*, a complete recovery. And every day I would ask myself, "Is he wounded? Did he survive the war? Is Barak ben Aurna still alive?'"

The waiter stood in the doorway of the suite, shocked but listening attentively. He broke into tears so touched that someone six thousand miles away was praying for him to survive and be well – to come home safely to his family. The husband hugged the waiter and the two parted.

This is a true story and very relevant for us now, because on Yom Kippur, when we do all this praying – and there's no day we do more praying than on Yom Kippur – we wonder: Is anyone paying attention? Are our prayers effective? Do they have an impact? Is God even listening?

Rabbi Joseph Soloveitchik explained that God always *hears* our prayers – He is a *shomea tefillah*, "one who listens attentively to our prayers." However, God isn't always a *mekabel tefillah*, "one who accepts our prayers favorably." We know that God does not always answer yes to our requests. Obviously, it can be a huge disappointment when God does not grant us our wishes, and in those situations we often assume God is simply not listening. However, Judaism believes God *always* listens. As with Moshe's entreaty to enter the land of Israel, God sometimes denies our requests but that does not mean He is ignoring them.

It is difficult to understand why God does not always answer our prayers as we would prefer, especially when those requests are critical, but it does not mean God isn't listening. I remember when my children were younger, and, on occasion, I would muster the strength to deny them one of their many requests. (I'm the pushover and my wife the disciplinarian.) My children's response was almost always, "Daddy, you're not listening!" And my response to them was always the same: "I *am* listening, I just don't think a sixteenth candy bar is a good idea right now!"

I do not mean to make light, but God – like any human parent –
is aware of the many more issues at stake and therefore has a broader
perspective on reality. A negative response to our prayers is therefore
not a reflection of a deaf or uncaring God, but of an all-knowing
Being privy to the infinite issues of which we are simply unaware.

And so, God always listens and our prayers matter. In the final
prayer service of Yom Kippur – in the *Ne'ilah* service – we say that
God takes all the tears from all of the prayers of the Jewish people
and puts them in a jar and saves them. God cherishes our prayers
and takes extra notice when we pour our hearts out.

Another Yom Kippur tradition expresses this beautifully.
Throughout the year, when we recite the *Shema* each day – "Hear
O Israel, the Lord is our God, the Lord is One" – we have a tradition
to whisper the next phrase in an undertone: *Baruch Shem Kevod
Malchuto Le'olam Va'ed*, "Blessed be the name of the glory of His
kingdom forever and ever." We whisper this line because, according
to tradition, when Moshe ascended Mount Sinai to receive the
Torah, he overheard the angels reciting this phrase: "Blessed be
the name of the glory of His kingdom forever and ever." After
Moshe overheard the phrase, he shared it with the people. And so,
in a sense, Moshe stole this line from the angels. And since, as the
Talmud teaches, just like a husband who steals jewelry for his wife
asks her not to wear it publicly, so too in regard to this stolen angelic
phrase, we too do not want to be too ostentatious with it. Thus, we
recite this celestial phrase – *Baruch Shem Kevod Malchuto Le'olam
Va'ed* – in an undertone.

But one day a year – on the day of Yom Kippur – we recite this
line aloud. After we recite the *Shema* declaration, we proudly yell
out: "Blessed be the name of the glory of His kingdom forever
and ever." What's different about Yom Kippur? On Yom Kippur
we are all considered angels. On this one day of the year, through

our prayers and observances, we transform ourselves into angelic beings. That is one of the reasons why on Yom Kippur we don't eat or drink and why on this day we minimize our physical activities. It's not because we are ascetic people, or that God will somehow look upon us more favorably if we cause ourselves to suffer. There is no such value in Judaism. Rather, we pull back from the physical world on Yom Kippur because it's the one day a year we remind ourselves that we *can* live as angels. That we can aspire to a greater and more lofty existence. It's the one day we remember that we are souls with a body and not just a body with a soul.

This Yom Kippur, when we deprive ourselves of food and drink, let us be reminded that we can aspire to more than *just* our physical existence. And as we mimic the angels by calling out "Blessed be the name of the glory of His kingdom forever and ever," may we merit to attain this high spiritual level, crying out to God and expressing our heartfelt prayers and knowing that, even if we don't get exactly what we want, God is always listening.

Question: Who is one other person on whose behalf you would like to pray for this Yom Kippur? Also, who is one person you would like to express gratitude to before Yom Kippur?

_____

_____

_____

_____

Day 38
Getting a 100%

YOM KIPPUR CAN FEEL LIKE A DAY OF ENDLESS PRAYING. The *machzor* – the prayer book we use on Yom Kippur – is thick and bulky, and it seems like we just keep praying all day. It can feel long and onerous, especially while fasting. But perhaps this year we can look at Yom Kippur differently – as a day to create a memory and a model for the rest of the year, a day for us to look back at and see how much we are capable of achieving and the spiritual heights we are able to reach.

I had a teacher – a rabbi in high school – who demanded a lot from his students. He always seemed to assign so much work. The homework, tests, and quizzes seemed endless and unmanageable, and it felt like no matter what I did, I couldn't keep up. Finally, after a few weeks, I decided to complain and tell my teacher that the workload was too heavy and it was time for him to switch me to a lower class level.

"You're Mark Wildes, right?" he said, looking at me. Meekly I answered, "Yes." "Didn't you receive a hundred on one of my tests?" he asked. Without waiting for me to respond, the rabbi opened his desk drawer and pulled out a test with my name on top next to a big "100%" written in red ink. Holding up my exam, he exclaimed: "Look at what you're capable of doing, Mark! You'll do just fine in this class, you got this."

Staring at the test with the 100 on it, I didn't have much of a response. So, I thanked the rabbi and walked away. I found out a few years later, that this was my teacher's strategy for all his students. He somehow figured out a way to make sure that, at some point in the year, every one of his students got a hundred on at least one test or quiz. That way, when any student would complain of the workload – as I did – he would pull out their 100 from his desk and show his student how capable they were of excelling in his class.

Yom Kippur is the day we all get a 100, not in terms of any grade God gives us, but a 100 in terms of how much we extend ourselves. It's the one day a year we live up to our full spiritual potential, so later in the year when we're feeling spiritually depleted – when we feel we are not capable of handling a certain spiritual challenge – we can look back at Yom Kippur and say, "Hey, that was me!" We can recall the way we stood and prayed for so long and say to ourselves: "Look how much focus and concentration I was able to muster on that day, even as I was fasting. Look at how devoted I was to my Judaism on that day. Maybe I can stay devoted now – even at this time of challenge."

This is one of the reasons we don't engage in physical activities on Yom Kippur. We don't eat or drink, nor do we engage in physical relations, because for this one day a year we transform ourselves into a more spiritual version of ourselves. We try to become like angels. Of course, Yom Kippur is a day to gain atonement for our sins and transgressions, but that's just one aspect of the day. It's also a day to create a memory and a model of our spiritual selves that we can look back at for inspiration the rest of the year. It is a day we can look back at ourselves and say, "I remember what I was like on Yom

Kippur. I remember how I transformed myself into such a spiritual being, so focused on my connection with God."

That is precisely why we have an *extra* prayer service on Yom Kippur called *Nei'lah*. Throughout the year we pray three times a day: *Shacharit* in the morning, *Mincha* in the afternoon, and *Ma'ariv* in the evening; and on Shabbat and the Festivals we add the *Musaf* service as well. On Yom Kippur however, we have an additional prayer that doesn't exist on any other day of the year. *Ne'ilah* is an add-on prayer, demonstrating our interest in extending ourselves beyond what we thought we were capable of.

Ne'ilah is short for *Ne'ilat She'arim*, which means the "closing of the gates." It represents the final prayers as Yom Kippur wanes, but it also represents how we push ourselves a little further. *Ne'ilah* means taking our Judaism to the next level, so we have this day to look back on, to recognize how holy, spiritual, and uplifted we can be. Then, when we are in the throes of a challenge, we can draw on the positive experience of Yom Kippur for strength.

There's a story told about a King of England who agreed to briefly ride his carriage through a small town on the outskirts of London. The people heard that the king was coming, and none were more excited than the children in the local orphanage. The caretakers bathed the children, dressed them in their finest clothes, and gave the children strict orders to stand at attention when they saw the king.

The day of the king's visit came, and everyone in the town assembled to watch the king. The little children lined up, well behaved, motionless, and silent. As the carriage passed by, one little boy broke ranks and ran up to the king's carriage! He climbed up the carriage and grabbed the king's lapel, holding up a picture of his parents. "These are my parents," the little boy cried, "I need you to save them!" The boy handed the king the picture and told him where he believed his parents were being kept.

The king was stunned by the break in protocol, but he admired the boy's passion to see his family. Moved by the child's zeal and intensity, the king decided to look into the matter, and eventually the king's advisors were able to reunite this orphan boy with his parents.

That is *Nei'lah*. It's the prayer when we break ranks, run up to the Almighty and grab Him by the lapels crying out, "Save us!" It's a moment when we show God – and ourselves – how passionate we are and what we're capable of. *Ne'ilah* is when we share our true feelings and in doing so attain great spiritual heights.

In the coming year, there will be times when we doubt ourselves and question if we can keep growing spiritually. Can we do that extra mitzvah or attend that Torah class after a long day of work? Can we refrain from hurtful gossip? Can we put on *tefillin*? Can we say a kind word to a friend who needs it? Can we light Shabbat candles on Friday night or show up on time to services on Shabbat morning? Can we pray once, twice, or even three times a day?

We can achieve what we're capable of or we can simply say to ourselves: "That's not me. I'm not that kind of Jew." Or we can look back to the way we were on this special day and say to ourselves: "On Yom Kippur, I *was* that kind of Jew. On Yom Kippur, I became that kind of spiritually elevated person – maybe I can do it now too."

Question: What is a spiritual goal that you currently feel is unachievable even though it's something you'd like to be able to accomplish? What tangible steps can you take towards achieving this goal?

_____

_____

_____

_____

Day 39
Reuniting the King and Queen
Erev Yom Kippur

RABBI JONATHAN SACKS, MAY HIS MEMORY BE A BLESSING, recalled the first time he met the Lubavitcher Rebbe – Rabbi Menachem Mendel Schneerson. Rabbi Sacks was a university student at Cambridge at the time and he was travelling to visit his aunt in Los Angeles. After he landed in New York, he tried to secure a meeting with the Rebbe before continuing on to California, but he was told such a meeting would be impossible. Undeterred, he left his phone number with one of the Rebbe's assistants, asking if a meeting would be possible.

On Saturday night, the young scholar, now with his aunt in California, received a phone call that a meeting could be arranged for that Thursday night. There wasn't enough time to book a flight, so the young Rabbi Sacks boarded a Greyhound and spent the next seventy-two hours riding a bus to meet the Rebbe at the Lubavitch headquarters at 770 Eastern Parkway in Brooklyn. Rabbi Sacks planned to ask the Rebbe some deep theological questions, the same questions he had asked many other prominent rabbis. But when he finally got to the meeting, the Rebbe instead started asking Rabbi Sacks some questions of his own: "How many Jewish students are there with you at Cambridge? How many of them are involved in Jewish life? What are you doing to bring your fellow Jewish students at Cambridge closer to their Jewish heritage?"

The meeting was *not* going as planned. Rabbi Sacks didn't travel all this distance to provide an update on Jewish life in Cambridge. So, he tried to bring the conversation back. "I did the English thing," said Rabbi Sacks in retelling the story. "The English can construct sentences like no one else can... we can construct more complex excuses for doing nothing than anyone else on earth, so, I started my answer with the following line: 'In the situation in which I currently find myself...' but the Rebbe wouldn't let him finish his sentence and cut in saying: 'Nobody finds himself in a situation. You put *yourself* in a situation, and if you put yourself in one situation, you can put yourself in a different one.'"

On Yom Kippur, we recite the confessionals – the *Al Chet* and the *Ashamnu*. Both prayers include a litany of sins and wrongdoings we have committed throughout the year. By reciting these confessionals and expressing remorse for our sins and mistakes, we take responsibility for our own actions. We could always say we *found* ourselves in this situation or we *found* ourselves in that situation, but instead we come clean before God and admit we *put* ourselves in this situation or *allowed* ourselves to be placed in another situation.

That is why Yom Kippur is this wonderful day of honesty and assuming responsibility. It's our time to admit that we're not just responsible for our micro-choices, but also the macro-choices that put us in those compromising situations to begin with.

Interestingly, the *Ashamnu* confession is written in alphabetical order. Why did the Sages list our sins and transgressions in the order of the Hebrew alphabet, beginning with the letter *aleph* and concluding with the letter *taf*?

The great Jewish novelist S.Y. Agnon offers the following parable: There was once a king who became displeased with his queen, banishing her from the palace to a faraway land. The queen missed the king terribly and yearned to be accepted back into the royal palace. And so, the queen took the same violin used years earlier at their wedding, and she played a beautiful melody for the king as she listed her wrongdoings, one by one. As the king listened to the music played on the special violin, he remembered his initial love for his bride, and welcomed her back to the palace with love and affection.

This parable represents the Jewish people's relationship with God. God, the King of Kings, grows unhappy with his queen, the Jewish people, because of their sins. The sins have caused spiritual distance resulting in the banishment of the queen, the Jewish people, from the palace. The violin is represented by the Hebrew alphabet – the letters used by God to give the Torah at Sinai. By means of the Hebrew alphabet, through which the Jewish people were wed to God at Sinai, and by which we sing letter by letter in the *Ashamnu* confessional, God and the Jewish people are reconciled.

Aleph, Bet, Gimel, Dalet.... We use the very letters from the giving of the Torah to arouse memories of our initial closeness with God at our wedding at Sinai. But ultimately, we take responsibility. We admit to God we have strayed, and that our sins have created spiritual distance from our Creator. We acknowledge our role in this, and at the same time we express our deep desire to be reunited and returned to the palace. The longing of the queen to be with the king motivates us to sing the *Al Chet* confessional with sincerity and passion.

Sincerity is the key to the *Ashamnu* and *Al Chet* confessions – which is why there are multiple mentions of sins in regard to speech. For example, we confess, "For the sin that we have sinned before You with confession of the mouth." This seems like a strange confession – aren't all prayers made with our mouths? Rebbe Meir of Apta (1776–1854) was asked this exact question by his students: Why is there a sin of confessing with our mouths? Isn't that exactly what we're supposed to be doing on Yom Kippur?

Rebbe Meir answered that when our confessions are *only* with our mouths, then it's a problem. A true confession must also be made with one's heart and mind. And so, as we recite the *Al Chet*, we ask God to forgive us for our insincere confessions – for those times we rush through the prayers and mindlessly mumble the words, and their profound ideas fail to penetrate into the recesses of our hearts. For that we must also atone.

Yom Kippur is all about being real and sincere. It's about acknowledging that we don't just *find* ourselves in certain situations. We put ourselves in those situations, or we allow ourselves to be placed in environments where we are more prone to compromise our values. As the Lubavitcher Rebbe told Rabbi Sacks: "If you put yourself in one situation, you can put yourself in a different one." On Yom Kippur, we take responsibility for the decisions we've made, and we celebrate our ability to make better ones in the year ahead. May that honesty and assumption of responsibility – together with our use of the Hebrew alphabet found in the confessionals – help reunite the King with His queen.

Question: What is one challenging or compromising situation in which you currently find yourself that seems like it "just happened" that, upon further reflection, you can take responsibility for? What possible change can you make in this area?

_____

_____

_____

_____

Day 40
A Broken Heart
Yom Kippur Day

THE JEWISH BLESSING OF *SHEHECHIYANU* – OF NEWNESS
and renewal – is recited whenever we do something new and special:
we wear a new article of clothing for the first time, we eat a fruit for
the first time in the season, or we perform a new holiday mitzvah like
the Seder on Passover, the *shofar* on Rosh Hashanah, or the shaking
of the *lulav* on Sukkot. On those special occasions, we praise God,
saying "Blessed are You, Lord our God, King of the Universe, who
has given us life, and sustained us, and delivered us to this season."

Interestingly, we also recite the *shehechiyanu* blessing of newness
and renewal on Yom Kippur. But why? What is new on Yom Kippur,
when there are no specific mitzvah objects associated with this
holiday?

The Belzer Rebbe answered that we recite the *shehechiyanu* on
Yom Kippur over our new selves, the new "us" that we are about to
become. After all, the point of Yom Kippur is to recreate ourselves
anew, becoming the very best version of ourselves.

Rambam makes the point in his "Laws of Repentance" that

teshuvah or returning to God enables us to become someone else. As we have discussed, the main part of the Yom Kippur service is the Thirteen Divine Attributes of Mercy. Throughout the day of Yom Kippur, we repeat these attributes numerous times. But why do we keep repeating these words? Is it all just hocus pocus? Is this just some divine formula that we mutter and all of sudden we're forgiven?

To answer this question, we need to remember one of the introductory phrases of the prayer, where we quote God's instructions to Moshe: "Anytime the Jewish people sin, they should *do* these Thirteen Attributes and I will forgive them." The key word here is "do." We're not simply *reciting* the Thirteen Attributes – we're "doing" them as well. We're living these prayers out. Our prayers are not simply words to be said, but rather ideas we ourselves become.

Let me leave you with a touching story to think about as you say another key prayer of Yom Kippur – the *Avinu Malkeinu*, "Our Father, our King." This true story is about a man who owned a fine jewelry store in Israel. One day, a nine-year-old girl walked into the store to buy a bracelet. She looked through the glass display case and pointed to an expensive piece of jewelry that cost about 16,000 shekels, which is almost four thousand dollars.

The owner of the store asked: "Do you want to buy that?"

"Yes," replied the nine-year-old girl.

"Well, you have very good taste, who do you want to buy it for?"

"For my older sister."

"That's very nice, but why do you want to buy your sister such an expensive bracelet?" asked the store owner.

"I don't have a father or a mother. My oldest sister takes care of all of us and so we collected all our money to buy her a present." With that comment, the nine-year-old girl pulled a handful of coins from her pocket. The jeweler counted up the change which amounted to seven shekels and eighty agurot – about two American dollars.

The storeowner was visibly moved and excitedly he told the little girl: "You're in luck! That's exactly what this bracelet costs." He wrapped the gift, handed the bracelet over to the little girl, who left the store with a big smile.

A few hours later, the older sister comes into the store and tells the owner: "I'm terribly sorry, sir. My little sister shouldn't have taken this bracelet without paying."

The owner said, "What are you talking about? It's paid in full."

"There's no way my sister could have afforded such a fine piece of jewelry," says the older sister.

"She paid in full" reiterated the store owner, "Seven shekels, eighty agurot, and a broken heart."

The store owner continued: "My wife died a few years ago. People come into my store every day to buy expensive pieces of jewelry and they can afford it. When your little sister walked in, wanting to buy you something special and then she showed me all the money she collected, it was the first time since my wife died that I remembered what it really means to love someone. So I gave her the bracelet and I wished her well."

On Yom Kippur, we will be making lots of requests from God. We will turn to Hashem on the holiest day of the year and we will ask Him for life, for good health, for a decent livelihood in the coming year. And then we will reach into our pockets to see what we've got to pay for all these beautiful blessings. And we will realize, maybe we have a few merits, but not enough to pay for all the things we're asking for. We will manage to pull out a few *shekalim*, a few dollars – a mitzvah here, a mitzvah there, a little Shabbat we observed, some charity we gave to the poor, we called someone who was lonely, we studied some Torah, we went to a few Jewish classes. But we don't really have what it takes to pay God for all the blessings for which we ask the Almighty on Yom Kippur. That's why the last line of the *Avinu Malkeinu* prayer begins, "Our Father, our King, have mercy on us and answer us, though we don't have enough deeds." We've accumulated a few merits over the year, but not enough to justify our request.

But we *do* have one thing, something we must never underestimate – a broken heart. "The Lord is near to the broken-hearted, and He saves those of crushed spirit" (Psalm 34:19). We come before God contrite and sincere, with a genuine interest in doing better in the year to come – to be kinder to our fellow human beings, to give more charity, to speak more positively about each other, to study more Torah, to increase our Shabbat observance. We conclude the *Avinu Malkeinu* with the words: "do with us charity and kindness and save us." We admit we don't have enough to pay for what we ask, O God, but please give us good health, please give us a life of sweetness and happiness. Do it in the merit of our broken heart – of us coming before You and saying: We know we can do better, just give us another chance.

In that merit – and in the merit of these forty days that we have spent studying Torah together and spiritually preparing for this holy time – may God inscribe us all for a new year of good health, prosperity, meaning, and purpose.

Shanah Tovah, my friends.

Question: Day 40! Congratulations. Identify three positive qualities within yourself. How in the next year can you make these virtues more of a permanent part of who you are?

_____

_____

_____

_____

The Day After

CONGRATULATIONS ON COMPLETING THE FORTY-DAY Challenge! I hope you were able to grow intellectually and spiritually from this process and that the few minutes of Torah you read each day added value and meaning to your High Holiday experience.

Just one parting message for you: On Day 13 of the Challenge, we raised the question, "What is the most important verse in the Torah?" I shared three responses by the great sages including Rabbi Shimon ben Pazzi's suggestion: "You shall offer one lamb in the morning, and the other lamb you shall offer in the afternoon" (Numbers 28:4). We discussed how at first glance this verse – referring to the daily offering in the Temple – seems pretty bland and uninspiring. But we then developed the idea of consistency – the value of sticking with something *every day*. We discussed how it may not always be so exciting to do the same thing day after day, but how that is precisely the way we accomplish the changes we want to see in our lives.

No matter how busy the Temple was, and no matter what else was going on, those two offerings were brought each day. Now that the High Holidays have concluded, what new activity can you commit to on a consistent basis? What new Jewish tradition or mitzvah can you introduce into your daily or weekly routine – that you can keep to – no matter what else is happening in your life?

It could be setting aside time to pray every day or starting your day by reciting the Morning Blessings to express gratitude for those things in life we take for granted. It could be lighting Shabbat candles or attending Shabbat services, visiting sick people in the hospital, volunteering for an important cause, giving charity on a more regular basis, reviewing the weekly Torah portion, or attending a Jewish class each week. Whatever it is you choose to do – consistency is the key. The routine of the everyday creates muscle memory and combats the sluggishness that inevitably sets in and keeps us from achieving our life goals. If we stop working out in the gym when we get tired, we just won't see progress. The results only come after we push through. That's how we become great, by doing whatever it is we want to become *every day*.

The Talmud tells the story of a poor person, a rich person, and a wicked person who come to heaven. Each was asked why they didn't study Torah. The poor man explained that he struggled to earn a living and had no time left over; the rich person defended himself, saying his business affairs drew him away; and the wicked man said he was very handsome and was constantly overcome by physical temptation. The heavenly tribunal answered by giving each person examples of even wealthier, poorer, and more handsome people who still managed to find time to study Torah (*Yoma* 35b). Now that the High Holidays are over, it's easy to return to business as usual and there will always be some "reason" why we don't have the time to develop our spiritual side. But if we want to become the very best version of ourselves, we must consistently integrate some new spiritual activity into our lives.

Those activities – really all of the 613 mitzvot of the Torah – whether it's refraining from speaking ill of others or reciting a blessing before we eat – are designed to change us and the world for the better. As I have tried to share in this book, mitzvot are not simply "things we do" but practices which deepen our connection to our fellow human beings and refine our personalities and behavior wherever we are – at work, at home, or just walking down the street. The Talmud explains that when one exhibits positive traits, the people around them will say, "Fortunate is his father who taught him Torah, fortunate is his teacher who taught him Torah" (*Yoma* 86a). When others see us acting in an elevated and ethical manner, it brings an added dimension of Godliness to the world. And on a deeper mystical level, when we observe a mitzvah, we create what the Kabbalists call a *dirah b'tachtonim* – a residence for God in the earthly realm. The mitzvah unlocks positive energy creating a more spiritually suitable environment for Hashem's presence to reside within ourselves and in the physical realm. Our mitzvot literally bring Godliness and His light into our world.

And so, although our forty days of Torah study has come to a close, our opportunity to bring the light of Torah into our world has just begun. Keep enjoying the journey!

About the Author

RABBI MARK WILDES is the Founder and Director of Manhattan Jewish Experience (MJE), a highly successful Jewish outreach and educational program that engages and reconnects unaffiliated Jewish men and women in their 20s & 30s with Judaism and the Jewish community. He is also the author of the highly acclaimed *Beyond the Instant: Jewish Wisdom for Lasting Happiness in a Fast-Paced Social Media World* (Skyhorse  Publishing, 2018). Rabbi Wildes earned a BA in Psychology from Yeshiva University, a Law Degree from the Cardozo School of Law, a Master's degree in International Affairs from Columbia University and ordination from the Rabbi Isaac Elchanan Theological Seminary (Yeshiva University).

After serving in rabbinic and outreach positions at Ohab Zedek and Kehilath Jeshurun and teaching at Ramaz and Stern College, Rabbi Wildes established MJE, dedicated to engaging the thousands of NYC's unaffiliated Jewish professionals. In its 22 years of existence, MJE has successfully reconnected thousands of previously unaffiliated Jewish men and women with Judaism and the Jewish community, hundreds of whom are today living committed Jewish lives and sending their children to Jewish Day Schools. Operating from its three locations in the city, with a talented staff of 15 professionals, MJE's inspirational Shabbat dinners, beginners services, retreats, educational classes, holiday events, and trips to Israel have touched the lives of thousands of young Jews and provided a venue through which 322 Jewish couples have married. Rabbi Mark also teaches an outreach training seminar at RIETS, Yeshiva University's rabbinical school, training new leaders for the future. He and his wife Jill and their 4 children live on the Upper West Side of Manhattan.